LEFTY ~
(KRIS... .....)
I HEAR YOU'RE AN
AGGIE AT HEART.
PAGE 10 IS FOR YOU.
WHOOP! GIG 'EM!
IN HIS EASY YOKE ~
Frank '65
PHIL 1:21

I Bleed MAROON

By Frank W. Cox III '65

FOREWORD BY RANDY MATSON '67

INSITE PRESS
BRYAN, TEXAS

Foreword

Through my work with Association of Former Students at Texas A&M University, I come into daily contact with Aggies. Each is a unique individual in his own right, but all share one common bond: the Aggie Spirit.

It is impossible to describe or explain Aggie Spirit, but from the day a student first steps onto campus and is greeted with a friendly, "Howdy!", he becomes a part of it. The Aggie Spirit fills each student and sets him apart from students of other institutions. Aggies support one another. They share each other's sorrows and joys, spoils and victories. One of my favorite examples dates back to 1968 when I was competing in the Olympics in Mexico City. Just before the finals in the shot, I received a "good luck" telegram from the student body at Texas A&M. It was 120 pages long with thousands of individual signatures. I was not alone in Mexico — each and every Aggie was behind me.

I Bleed Maroon is a book inspired by stories such as these. It's a book about what it means to be an Aggie. Taking you back to the campus as it was in the Sixties, Frank Cox walks us through the Aggie Experience as he lived it, as I lived it, and as anyone attending A&M today lives it. A clever mix of history, trivia and personal recollections, you will find yourself rediscovering — or discovering for the first time — what it really means to be an Aggie. I hope you will enjoy, *I Bleed Maroon* as much as I did.

Randy Matson '67
Executive Director,
Association of Former Students

Dedication

First, I would be amiss if I did not start with my Heavenly Father who has blessed me in so many ways — one of which was allowing me to attend Texas A&M. Then my mom and dad, who never had the opportunity to go to college but who were determined to see that I did. They sacrificed their own desires and pleasures in order that I could partake of the joys of Aggieland. I could not leave out my wife, Cheryl, who also could not attend A&M as a student but who is a true Aggie in every sense of the word. It is good to have a spouse who enjoys the fellowship of my Aggie friends as much as I. My son, John, Class of '95, and daughter, Cristy, Class of '98, have loved everything about being an Aggie from day one. I only hope their days at A&M are as rewarding and fulfilling as mine.

And, then, there are the parents of my Aggie friends whom I grew to love and appreciate so much. You have had a tremendous impact on my life. I dedicate this book to all of you, the sons and daughters of Texas A&M.

Acknowledgments

Aggies throughout the ages are responsible for the contents of this book. Without their devotion and service to Texas A&M and its traditions, there would be nothing to write about. Thank you and GIG 'EM!

My appreciation goes out to my wife, my son, my daughter, my mother and my aunt who have loved me through it all. Also, thanks to my cousins John and Blair Case who reviewed, edited and made many improvements to the contents of *I Bleed Maroon*. I love each of you.

Admiration to Aggie Harry H. Elliott '60, a life-long victim of cerebral palsy, for being an inspiration to me as a young boy growing up in New Boston, Texas.

To those of you who endorsed my book with your positive statements, I am grateful and honored by your support.

Thanks to Cliff Dugosh and Dan Debenport for letting me include your poems in the book.

To the families of Peggy Potter, Steve Case, Corey Tompkins, Susan Routh, Darryl Taylor, David Franklin, Joe Dawson, Barbara Taylor and Patricia Cannon — thank you for your prayers in this effort. Brigette Bickham, Wendy Brothers, Stacy Doss, Mark Morgan, Rob Potter, Julie Reams and Kiersten Taylor — thanks for your enthusiastic encouragement and support.

And, finally, Allison Seale, Debbie Harris, and Carolyn Wilkins, I remain amazed at your ability to read, interpret, translate, and transform my handwritten notes and drafts into a typed manuscript. Your patience is admired and appreciated.

To those of you who purchase *I Bleed Maroon*, you can know that through an agreement with the publisher, the author, and the administration of Texas A&M University, a portion of the profits from each book goes directly to the furtherance of the spirit and traditions which have made Texas A&M the special place that it is.

Thank you and God bless you all!

—AGGIELAND—
"Why I Love Her So"

You ask me why
I love her so,
  Absorb this poem
and then you'll know.

Have you listened to the clinking
of spurs on the senior's boots;
  Or sought out the history and legends
of the Aggie's family roots?

Have you watched the band and corps
outside the famed old dorm,
  Assemble and "dress right dress"
until a straight line is formed?

Have you ever noticed when
"Old Glory" is unfurled,
  How a sense of victory and pride
does about them swirl?

Have you felt the firm grip
of their strong hand-shake?
  Have you wondered where we find
these young men to make?

Have you watched the 12th Man
stand throughout the game,
  Always one for all and all for one;
each different, yet all the same?

Have you listened at "Silver Taps"
when the RV rifles blast the night,
  And the deadly silence is broken
as the birds take off in flight?

Have you been present when
the "Muster Roll" they call,
  For those who've passed away,
one by one 'til they've called us all?

Elephant walk, bonfire, corps trips
and midnight yell too,
  Where do they find the study time
and yet all this do?

Have you stood at Final Review
for the senior's last march-by?
  Have you seen them salute their friends
with a tear in their eye?

Have you considered the Aggie thousands
who lived and fought and died,
  So that you and I, in freedom,
can enjoy all of America's pride?

It must come from somewhere,
deep within,
  The same spirit and devotion
that causes us in life to win.

Why, we've won at Austin, Corregidor,
and Iwo Jima too,
  And in Korea, Vietnam and Desert Storm—
we always do!

Don't you know?
Haven't you seen or heard?
  We're the Aggies, the Aggies are we—
true to our word.

Well, I have!
Why I've been there for it all!
  And I'll remember it yet,
even past my own muster's call!

Why it's Aggieland—
where I met my best and life-long friends,
  The ones who've loved me in spite,
of my failures and my sins.

It's where I've always
most longed to be!
  Yes, it's Aggieland, there,
for you and for me.

If it weren't for heaven,
Aggieland is where I'd want to spend eternity,
  There with my family & Aggie buddies, who,
except for Jesus, have been the closest to me.

Now, do you see why
I love her so?
  You should! It's all over me!
It's that Maroon Aggie glow!

—Frank W. Cox, III,[65] 21April91
(author of *I Bleed Maroon*)

Table of Contents

Introduction

There is so much to write and to tell — so many good memories. Yet, I went into this effort knowing I had an impossible task — because, as you know, "There is a Spirit that can ne'er be told . . ." I am sure most of you have had thoughts about writing a book about your days at Aggieland but have not gotten around to it. Well, I finally made myself get around to it.

As you will see from reading *I BLEED MAROON*, I am not a professional writer by any means. However, I did want to express some of my thoughts and memories on paper — something to pass on to Ags of all ages — sort of a long over due "thank you" note to Texas A&M. Though I mostly wrote in the first person and about personal experiences (I knew of no other way), it is, nonetheless, my hope and intent that through your reading of *I BLEED MAROON* that those of you who are Aggies will be reminded of *your* class, *your* friends, *your* experiences. For you future Ags, my mission will be accomplished if, through the reading of this book, you gain an awareness and appreciation for the Aggies who have preceded you and a desire to become totally involved and protective of the traditions and spirit that make Aggieland the special place that it is. In fact, it will tickle me maroon if you become so side-tracked and engrossed in your own memories and future possibilities that, by the time you finish the book, you will be saying, "I could have written that. Just change the names and the dates, and it describes (or will describe) me and my days at Aggieland!"

Since I scarcely knew where to start, I decided to start in the same way my favorite Author started my favorite Book . . . .

Chapter 1

In The Beginning

"IT SEEMS Like Only Yesterday" — the Berlin Wall had just gone up in August, and the Bay of Pigs Invasion had been just six months before. Most of us had never heard of the small Southeast Asian country called South Vietnam which, in just a few short years, would play such an important role in our lives.

"West Side Story" won the Oscar for Best Picture and Andy Williams' "Moon River" won a Grammy. Arnold Palmer captured The British Open and Gary Player won The Masters. Floyd Patterson was the Heavyweight Champion of the world.

George Bush was working in the oil fields of West Texas, and Nolan Ryan was "throwing heat" in his home town of Alvin. Roger Maris hit 61 homers to break Babe's record. The Yankees won the Series. Twenty years earlier Ted Williams became the

last ball player to hit over 400. Alan Shepard Jr. became
America's first man in space.

Rock & Roll, "Twist & Shout," the Bop, the Stroll, '57
Chevys, T-Birds, flat tops, and bobby socks were still the rage.
Roy Orbison's "Running Scared" (we fish could certainly
identify with that) was at the top of the charts. "Pretty Woman"
was not in sight for Orbison or Aggieland at the time. Chuck
Berry, The Big Bopper, Rickey Nelson, Conway Twitty — my
kids think we had it made; I believe we did.

The population of Bryan/College Station was less than
30,000, and the price of gasoline fluctuated around 24 cents a
gallon. The enrollment at A&M hovered around 8,000 students who were mostly Texans. Participation in the corps was
compulsory for two years, and there were no females for miles.

Kevin Costner was six. Elvis was twenty-six and the "King
of Rock & Roll." And I was in love with Natalie Wood. Yet, to

Texas A&M Campus Then

me and my fish buddies, other events would soon fill our hearts and minds with memories never to be forgotten, memories similar to the ones going through your mind right now.

The year was 1961. Like most kids from small Texas towns — towns like New Boston, Van Vleck, DeKalb, Alvin, Mart, Hondo, and Gonzales   I went to A&M as a green and unsuspecting boy of 18. Yes, I soon found out I was not too different from those kids from Houston, Dallas, and San Antonio. None of us could have dreamed of what was ahead. It was a good thing because most of us would not have gone to Aggieland in the first place had we had an inkling of what lay in store for us during our fish year. I am glad we didn't know because many of us would have missed out on the best years of our lives.

We arrived in September in the midst of one of the worst hurricanes in Texas history, Hurricane Carla. While your class might not have descended upon Aggieland riding the wings of a storm, I'm sure you knew something was brewing as soon as you stepped foot on the campus. Little did we realize, at the time, that the fury of the storm was mild compared to the fury of those hungry, mean, and less-than-understanding sophomores who came to be known as "wet-heads" (or something like that). This was a very appropriate term for them, but that is another story . . . back to the beginning.

After haircuts, uniform issue, and dorm assignments, we finally arrived at our home-away-from home — in my case, Dorm 6, Room 106. It was there I began my journey to becoming a life-long, maroon-bleeding, fightin' Texas Aggie.

There we were, three of us in a room big enough for one, stacked on top of each other in a three-section bunk bed. Being the shortest, I was assigned the top bunk. I still have bumps on my head from hitting the ceiling when the "Whistle Jock" would blow, "first call for chow, fall out for chow...!" It did not take long to realize that this was not exactly how college life was depicted in the current Sandra Dee movie showing at the Wakea Theater in New Boston when I left home. I was beginning to think that maybe my mom was right after all. She had wanted me to go to Baylor. (Don't hiss her too loudly, she became one of the all-time great Aggie supporters before my first semester ended — just like all Aggie moms.)

In our "Easy Come Easy Go" Gator 2 Squadron, we had two "wet-heads" who looked exactly alike — at least to us fish. They were both skinny, short, and blond. It was not until the end of the first semester that we could tell them apart. (It is hard to see clearly when you mix tears with fear.) They, Bill Frels and Ed Tomlin, gave us fits, along with R. Lee Reavis, who was the "Motorcycle King" of Squadron 2. What a trio. And the Kingston Trio thought they had something special — they just did not know about the Gator 2 Trio. (Mr. Frels·became a successful businessman in Houston and continues to be a staunch supporter of Texas A&M. Mr. Reavis has served our country for more than 25 years as a Colonel in the United States Air Force and returns to Aggieland as often as possible. I am ashamed to say I have lost track of "Mr. Tomlin, Sir.")

Then came our first "big" event — "All College Night." And it was just that, because it was the first time that all students were gathered together in one place. The site was G. Rollie White Coliseum, the "Holler House on the Brazos." I will never forget it — what a night. After marching to G. Rollie and "wildcatting" into the coliseum, we fish, all khaki clad with shaved heads, took our place in the stands on the west side of the gymnasium. Talk about everybody looking alike! There we were — Ted, David, Johnnie, Herb, Ron, Steve, Larry, Roy, Buddy, Malon, George, ... But on that day in 1961, we were all just plain ol' fish Jones. What a class, the Class of '65 (much like yours) — "All for one and one for all." Anyway . . .

That's when the head yell leader, Jim Davis, Class of '62, jumped on the platform and looked all of us fish in the eye. (I'm sure you Aggies remember how it seemed; it was just as if he were looking straight at you.) Then, he said, "I want you to look at the man on your right and the man on your left because he won't be here at the end of the year." I thought to myself that what he said was at least a half-truth because I wasn't even going to be here at the end of the week, much less the end of the year. Why, my "fish ol' lady" (roommate) hadn't even unpacked yet! (Don't laugh too hard, you probably hadn't unpacked either.)

Nobody had ever made me feel so low and unworthy as those upperclassmen did. Even marching was a test of survival. I had never marched in my life. They kept telling me to "dig-in" my left heel on "utt." The problem was every sound the First Sergeant made in calling cadence sounded like "utt." I always wondered, but never asked, if all my fish buddies thought the same thing. I was beginning to wonder why I was paying my hard- earned money to be treated like that. Of course, we know now that the cost was infinitesimal in comparison to what we received. But that wasn't what I was thinking as he was yelling "utt." Frankly, I was still too scared to move. Well, back to "All College Night". . . .

The head yell leader began to introduce the football team and coaches. He taught us a few yells and talked about what it meant to be an Aggie. I listened to every word. Then it happened! For the first time, as a member of the Twelfth Man, I participated in the singing of "The Spirit of Aggieland." I was "gigged" from then on. That's not to say I never felt like leaving again, because I did — especially on a Saturday night when the upperclassmen would pass by our windows with their dates. I probably would have hit Highway 6 in a hurry if it hadn't been for the encouragement given to me by former A&M Regent Norman Moser '37, Lin Wilson '63, Clyde Bickham '63, Greg

Garcia '62, Dick Hickerson '61, Randy Wortham '61, and Randy's wife, Lynda. Just when I was about to be "down for the count," they would come to lift me up, doing all the things older Ags have done for younger Ags throughout the existence of A&M. What a tradition! What a school!

It was rough, challenging, trying, testing, hard, almost impossible—but the oneness, the togetherness, the comradeship, the esprit de corps overwhelmed those of us who stayed. It was great! Yep, the blood was at least mauve at this point and getting deeper maroon by the day.

Chapter 2

What is an Aggie Anyway?

IT SEEMS that no matter where one goes outside of Aggieland, there are always those who ask, "What is an Aggie anyway?" I am so glad they ask because it gives me an opportunity to talk about one of my favorite subjects.

I usually respond by first telling them what an Aggie is *NOT*. An Aggie is not a pig or hog, as they are called in the Ozarks. An Aggie is not a horse, such as the one representing that school out in West Texas. An Aggie is not a pony, like the one in "SMUland." We are certainly not a frog or horned toad, nor a Waco bruin or bear. We are not a little ol' cat or a fowl owl like those in Houston. Most definitely, we are not of the long-horned cattle variety. If we were, we would be a bull or a cow rather than some non-productive steer. (Since a steer is non-productive, and t.u. chooses to be represented by a steer, then logic would follow that t.u. must consider themselves . . . . Hey, don't get mad at me or say, "that's a little strong;" I didn't pick their mascot, they did.)

The fact is that an Aggie is not any type of animal. We have Reveille, who is our 1st Lady, but we're not the Texas A&M Reveilles. We're the Aggies. An Aggie is a human. When I think of an Aggie, I think of church, community, and state leaders. I think of the many Aggies who have sacrificed their lives as defenders of freedom through their service to the United States of America.

More Aggies served as Reserve Officers in World War II than did students from any other school, including the military academies. From the Class of 1945 alone, 106 men gave their lives in the defense of their country. And many Aggies, such as James Ray '63, have been Prisoners of War. Ray was a POW during the Vietnam War for more than six years. He credits his faith and his experience as an Aggie cadet as the reason he was able to survive and return to Texas A&M as an employee of the campus today. Others have been the very first in battle. Col. L.D. "Don" Holder Jr. '66 spearheaded the advance of Allied Forces by sweeping through Southern Iraq and Kuwait as he commanded the 2nd Armored Calvary Regiment in the Persian Gulf War of 1991. Col. George Walton '71 flew the first sortie into Iraq; Col. John Sylvester '67 commanded the Tiger Tank Brigade, and Col. Randolph House '67 commanded the Black Jack Tank Brigade in Operation Desert Storm. We only had four of our tanks hit while we destroyed 4,000 of Iraq's. More than 250 Aggies served in the Persian Gulf War. Three gave their lives — Richard Price '74, Danny Hull '81, and Thomas "Cliff" Bland '86. Though I mention only a few by name, there are thousands more whose service and dedication have been just as in ensuring our freedom. It is easy to see why the saying, "Join the Army and help the Texas Aggies win the war," became a recruiting theme. How true it is!

Major General Thomas G. Darling, Class of 1954, served his country for more than 30 years in a variety of leadership positions in the United States Air Force prior to assuming the position of the commandant of the Corps of Cadets at Texas A&M in 1987.

One of our most distinguished presidents of A&M, Earl Rudder '32, led the Rangers against the German forces on Omaha and Utah Beaches in World War II. General George F. Moore '08 was the heroic defender of Corregidor in World War II. And it was General George Patton who said, "Give me an army of West Point graduates, and I'll win a battle. Give me a handful of Texas Aggies, and I'll win the war."

More than 150 Aggies have advanced to the rank of general, and eight Aggies have been presented the nation's highest honor, the Congressional Medal of Honor. One recipient, William G. Harrell, won his medal for continuing to fight in spite of a broken thigh and the loss of both hands during the invasion of Iwo Jima in World War II. In 1943, a full length movie, *"We've Never Been Licked,"* was made about Texas A&M to show the world the story of Aggieland and the dedication and service of its graduates.

Aggies are the first to answer the call to serve their country. Aggies are ministers of the gospel, coaches of Little League teams, public school teachers, and leaders in community projects. Many are medical doctors, veterinarians, and engineers. Others are civil servants, congressmen, and entrepreneurs. Thankfully, many are responsible for feeding the world as farmers, ranchers, and agricultural researchers. And we all know that if it were not for Aggies who become lawyers, there wouldn't be such a thing

as a "good" lawyer. In essence, Aggies get things done. We are
doers! Aggies are the Twelfth Man, builders of bonfires, carriers
of tradition, participants in Musters, and, too often, attenders of
Silver Taps ceremonies. Texas Aggies say *HOWDY.* We know
how to look a man in the eye and shake hands. Aggies get a chill
up our spine when we hear the National Anthem or sing the
"Spirit of Aggieland" or "Aggie War Hymn," or when we march
to chow under the direction of a drum and bugle corps.

While there are a few students at A&M who are not true
Aggies, there are many Aggies who were never students at
A&M. Their love of and dedication to the students and
traditions of Texas A&M make them Aggies. As a supreme
example of this, though not graduates of A&M, Dr. John
Koldus and his lovely wife Mary Dell have served as 'away-from-
home' parents to thousands of Aggies for almost 20 years. Dr.
Koldus is the top Assistant to the President of Texas A&M
University and is the only person who has ever received the two
most prestigious awards given by the National Association of
Student Administrators. Now, tell me they aren't Aggies in the
truest sense. They represent what Texas A&M is all about.
Another example is that of Dick and Pat Brunner who were the
1990 Aggie Parents of the Year. Dick graduated from another
university years ago; but he has a burning desire to have an Aggie
Ring of his own. Therefore, Dick travels 90 miles (one-way) to
attend classes at Texas A&M. It might take a few years to get the
ring, but it will be well worth the wait. All Aggies can agree with
that!

Aggies are loyal, trustworthy, and dedicated. Aggies are
true friends. The following story kind of sums it all up. My
daughter, Cristy, was thirteen when she went to Dallas with a
friend and her family for a weekend trip. Cristy went walking
through the restaurant wearing her Aggie tennis shoes and

socks, Aggie shorts, Aggie top, and an Aggie ribbon in her hair. As they were looking for tables, two old Ags from the Class of '41 were sitting at a table and saw her. Of course, they said, "GIG 'EM," and threw up their thumbs. Cristy immediately went to their table and hugged them and carried on a long conversation with them. Cristy's friend couldn't believe that she would go up and talk to a couple of strangers. Cristy told her that they weren't strangers, they were Aggies. Yep, Aggies are truely 'something else!'

What is an Aggie? Who are the Aggies? It is simple, "We are the Aggies, the Aggies are we, true to each other as *only* Aggies can be . . . ."

AGGIES - HOW SPECIAL!

Chapter 3

Poor Aggies? No Way, Never!!

"POOR AGGIES," the t.u. students say. How ridiculous and little of them. Yet, how appropriate that it should come from them. If they only knew or would only accept the truth, how different they might be.

For a student or supporter of a so-called "institute of higher learning" to say, "Poor Aggies," only derides and belittles that person and institute. But then, t.u.'s school song never even once mentions their school. Teasips, staying true to form, even stole the tune for their song from "I've Been Working on the Railroad." Why, we even had to help them name their mascot! (For those who don't know, in 1915 A&M beat t.u. 13-0 and branded the score on the t.u. mascot. The "teasips," in an attempt to cover up their embarassment, made a "B" out of the "13," an "E" out of the hyphen, inserted a "V," and left the

"O." Thus, the name, BEVO.) It is a matter of record that their school song was written as a protest against their president. For them ever to say anything bad about another school is ludicrous.

In contrast, A&M's fight song, "The Aggie War Hymn," was written by J.V. "Pinky" Wilson during World War I while standing guard on the Rhine River. Our school song, "The Spirit of Aggieland," was written by Aggie student Marvin Mimms and Colonel Richard Dunn in 1925. Knowing all these facts, it is hard to believe that some people think that one school is as good as another. We Ags know better. We've always known better! (It may be hard to believe, but I, like some of you, do have several good friends and even some relatives who went to t.u. They basically are conservative, love America and are good citizens and servants in their communities. They just weren't aware of the differences between the schools before they assigned their loyalty.) I recently read where A&M and t.u. are joining together for some research efforts. Well, all I can say is that in research there is always a lot of "trial and error." So, I suppose we'll do the trial and let t.u. do the error. Sounds good to me.

"Poor Aggies," they say. It's kind of sad to think they just don't know; for in truth, we are *rich*. Oh, maybe not all of us in a financial or material way — though I would stack us up against t.u., and anyone else, in that realm as well. We are rich in other ways, more important ways. Such as in *TRADITION*: Aggie rings, senior boots and sabres, Midnight Yell Practice, corps trips, the Twelfth Man, Howdy, Reveille, and "Whipping Out." What other student body stands throughout a game to show support for their team or holds a yell practice following a game in which we happen to be outscored? How many have had a full-length movie made about them as we have in "We've Never Been Licked"? Who comes close to building a bonfire that compares to ours? What other campus is so friendly or has a student body so disciplined? *NONE!* And to think, it only happens in *Poor*(?) Aggieland!

We are also rich in *DEDICATION*: Yes, we're extremely wealthy in expressing our love in unique ways: such as we do by having "Silver Taps" when a fellow Aggie departs this life, or to "Muster" together on April 21 each year, gathering with friends in foxholes or homes to have a final roll call for a departed comrade of Aggieland. What university has provided more officers to serve our nation in time of need? What school has produced more Congressional Medal of Honor winners? While others riot and burn and loot, we fight and serve to protect the peace and freedom Americans hold dear. Unashamedly, we show respect and devotion to God, Country, Family, and Flag.

Yes, again and again we are proud patriots of honor and duty. "Some may boast of prowess bold, of the school they think so grand, but there is a spirit can ne'er be told, it's the spirit of Aggieland."

Poor Aggies? If so, let us remain so forever. Poor? Oh, no! Never! Not in any way, form, or fashion. For you see, we "stand united — that's the Aggie theme, We're the Twelfth Man on the fightin' Aggie team."

No, I wouldn't have it any other way. After all, we are the Aggies.

Chapter 4

Aggie History and Traditions

IT WOULD be impossible to cover all Aggie Traditions. However, a few which mean so much to all sons and daughters of A&M are included below.

History

A&M was established as the first public institution of higher education under the Morrill Act of July 2, 1862. On September 17, 1876, the Agricultural and Mechanical College of Texas was officially opened for registration. The school officially began classes on October 2, 1876 with a total of six students. Today, we average around 41,000 students at Texas A&M University, including over 6,800 graduate students. The A&M physical plant is valued at approximately $1 billion. The campus in

College Station includes 5,142 acres and is the largest campus of any major institution of higher education in the nation.

The University is one of only three institutions with a full time Corps of Cadets, including ROTC programs leading to commissions in all four branches of the military service — Army, Air Force, Navy, and Marine Corps.

Texas A&M's extensive research efforts in all fields in 1988-89 totaled about $250 million. This was more than any other university in Texas and among the top ten universities throughout the nation.

In 1971, Texas A&M was designated as a Sea Grant University in recognition of its achievements in oceanographic and marine resources development. Texas A&M was one of the first four institutions in the nation to achieve this distinction. In 1989, Texas A&M University was designated a Space Grant University.

Texas A&M continues to grow and excel in its quest for excellence in providing dedicated, proven leaders for the challenges that face the free world as we head into the 21st century.

The Aggie Spirit

We are a part of the gallant fighting spirit which Aggies have always displayed. Aggie Spirit is part of our daily life. It is this spirit that inspires A&M men and women everywhere with a feeling of unity and undying devotion to our school.

Aggie Spirit defies definition. Aggie loyalty attaches itself so firmly that we will carry it with us the rest of our lives. Aggie Spirit molds character; it comes from within. Once an Aggie, always an Aggie. From the outside looking in, you can't understand it. From the inside looking out, you can't explain it. But it's real!

Yes, it is associated with all of the traditions, the campus, the buildings, the ball games, and the events. Yet, it mostly has to do with the Aggies, the friends, the parents, and the people who make up Aggieland.

The Twelfth Man

The tradition of the Twelfth Man was born the second of January, 1922, when an underdog Aggie team was playing Centre College, then the nation's top ranked team. As the hard fought game wore on, and the Aggies dug deeply into their limited reserves, Coach D.X. Bible remembered a squad man who wasn't in uniform. King Gill was called from the stands, suited up, and stood ready throughout the rest of the game, which A&M finally won 22-14.

Photo from Texas A&M University Archives

The Twelfth Man

Although Gill didn't play in the game, he had accepted the call to help his team. He came to be thought of as the Twelfth

Man because he stood ready for duty in the event that the eleven men on the gridiron needed assistance. That spirit of readiness for service, desire to support, and enthusiasm to help kindled a flame of devotion among the entire student body; a spirit that has grown vigorously through the years. All Aggies feel loyal to our school. All stand throughout an Aggie game, ready for duty, if called. The entire student body at A&M is the Twelfth Man.

The tradition is so unique that it is included as an example of how "one can come out of nowhere to win respect" in the *New International Version Of The Student Bible,* Psalm 113.

The Yell Leaders

Selected by the student body, these five Aggies lead the Twelfth Man in the singing of the school songs and the yells. Yell Leaders are selected to these highly visible positions because of their knowledge of all the traditions, songs, and yells and because of their love of A&M. They are responsible for control of the crowd and for helping to teach young Ags about the spirit of Aggieland and its traditions.

The Yell Leaders, comprised of three seniors and two juniors, perform at games, yell practices, and corps trips. They also participate in Fish Camp and Freshman Orientation. They are considered the "Keepers of the Spirit" of Aggieland.

Yell Leaders first performed at A&M in the early 1920's. Originally, the upperclassmen made the fish do yells during game half-times. The story goes that the freshman Yell Leaders were getting so much attention from the upperclassmen's dates that the juniors and seniors decided they had better get in on a little of the action. They decided to put the fish back in the stands, and they elected juniors and seniors to Yell Leader positions. Yep, rank does have its privileges.

The Yell Leader's high-stepping strut came about from the natural tendency to step high and softly when walking through numerous and hazardous "cow patties" that were scattered randomly about the campus during the early days of the predominantly agricultural school. All just another example of the uniqueness of all aspects of Texas A&M.

The Singing Cadets

This widely known and highly talented singing group consists of more than 50 Aggie voices. Membership is selected from the entire student body after tryouts. The Singing Cadets annually appear before many Texas high school and college audiences and in communities and churches throughout the state, nation, and world.

The Singing Cadets

The Fightin' Texas Aggie Band

The Aggie Band, comprised of approximately 300 cadets, is the largest marching military band in the world. They are often referred to as the "pulse" of the Spirit of Aggieland. The band supplies music for football, basketball, and baseball games, as well as for yell practices, corps trips, and military functions.

The Ross Volunteer Company

This unit was organized in 1887 by Colonel T. M. Scott for the purpose of banding together the most proficient military men at A&M into a crack drill team. The name, Ross Volunteers, was selected in 1891 to honor ex-Governor Lawrence Sullivan Ross who became president of Texas A&M in that same year. RV's serve as the honor guard for the Governor of Texas and for "King Rex" at Mardi Gras in New Orleans each year. They also perform for many other special events throughout the year on the A&M campus.

Membership is restricted to approximately 90 outstanding cadets chosen from among the junior and senior classes. New members are elected into the Ross Volunteers each year.

Parson's Mounted Cavalry

The horse cavalry program was originally formed in 1919 at Texas A&M as part of the program to commission reserve officers into the cavalry branch. The horse cavalry flourished at A&M from 1919 until the demise of the cavalry in the United States Army in 1943. In 1973, the Aggies mounted up once again when some men with a love of tradition and imagination helped to reform the unit at A&M.

Rudder's Rangers

Rudder's Rangers is an organization composed of 50 to 75 volunteers. It is designed to provide highly motivated cadets the opportunity to develop further leadership traits. The company is named in memory of Major General Earl Rudder who was a Texas A&M graduate, past president of the A&M system, commander of the 2nd Ranger Battalion in World War II, and holder of the Distinguished Service Cross. The specific objectives of the organization are to prepare its members for Ranger School, ROTC Advanced Camp, and to develop leadership potential.

Fish Drill Team

Only freshmen are eligible for this elite team. Even then, only the most disciplined and determined choose to complete

Fish Drill Team

the entire year. At the end of the year, those who have persevered
are awarded a drill team cord and citation medal which symbolize
hard work, integrity, and strong self-discipline.

During the year, the freshmen have the opportunity to travel
to drill meets around the nation and to display the discipline and
precision that has earned the team national recognition.

Military Training And Service

Military training has been offered at A&M since the institution was established. Since that time, the sons of A&M have
continued to use the talents they gained through their military
training in all battles for freedom. In April of 1917, the Class of
1917 left school practically en masse and enrolled in the Officer
Training School for World War I. The Class of '42 joined the
more than 6,000 Aggies already in service at the beginning of
World War II, bringing the total to 18,000 Aggies — 13,000 of
whom were officers — serving in the "War To End All Wars."
This was more than any other school, including the military
academies.

Some 5,000 additional reserve officers were trained and
commissioned at A&M. Another 7,000, who had received some
military training at A&M, were commissioned through Officer's
Candidate School and answered the call to arms. Six thousand
more served effectively as the direct result of A&M training,
most of them as non-commissioned officers. The service of
these 18,000 Aggies did much to enhance the brilliant record of
A&M, as well as to uphold the tradition of the "Fighting
Texan." All Aggie veterans have served gallantly, many have
received medals, and eight Aggies have won the Congressional
Medal of Honor.

During the early stages of World War II, General Douglas

Photo from Texas A&M University Archives

Major General Earl Rudder
President of Texas A&M 1959 - 1970

MacArthur wrote: "Texas A and M is writing its own military history in the blood of its graduates . . . . No name stands out more brilliantly than the heroic defender of Corregidor, General George F. Moore. Whenever I see a Texas man in my command, I have a feeling of confidence."

General Eisenhower, speaking at the Victory Homecoming in 1946 declared: "I feel only a lasting admiration for the Texas A&M Corps of Cadets. This admiration extends to the individual, as well as to the institution that produced you."

"At Texas A&M," General Omar Bradley told the 1950 June graduating class, "there has been an almost unlimited opportunity for you in science, in agriculture and veterinary medicine, in engineering, and arts. In true Texas tradition, you have been provided with outstanding training in military science, in aeronautical science, and in physical education. The men of Texas A&M can stand up to any men in the world and compare favorably their education and training for leadership — leadership in the pursuits of peace, and if it comes to war, leadership in battle. This combination is significant, for the capability for a productive peace, coupled with the ability to defend your beliefs, as well as your resources, is essential to survival."

Perhaps former A&M President T. O. Walton summed up their feelings and dedication when he said in "The Cadence" of 1942, "Time is the element of which life is made .... You have no right to waste your time because your talent and your ability are needed in the service of society and your country."

Texas A&M University today has one of the most comprehensive programs of military science in the nation. It enrolls the largest Corps of Cadets of any military college in the United States and is the nation's largest single source of trained officer reserves for the Army, Air Force, and Navy. Over 20,000 Aggies have served as officers in the military service.

These records and tributes by military leaders of our time bear witness to the fact that A&M has served well in all battles for freedom including World War I, World War II, Korea, Vietnam, and Operation Desert Storm. Aggies continue to meet the goals set out for A&M by its designers — to serve "as the strength and shield of civil liberties."

Memorials

Most Aggie memorials, past, present and future, are displayed in the hearts of Aggies throughout the world. However, as one might expect from a university rich in military tradition, there are numerous memorials on the A&M campus. Locations of these memorials are described in another Aggie book, *Footsteps: A guided tour of the Texas A&M University campus*, by Jerry C. Cooper, '63 and Henry C. Dethloff, published by Texas A&M University Press. The following is a list of some of the memorials and their histories:

✬ The Memorial Student Center (MSC) was originally dedicated to the 918 Aggies who died in the defense of our country in World War II. There is also a plaque to honor the 104 Aggies "who led and supported us during the gallant defense of Bataan and Corregidor from 8 December, 1941, to 6 May, 1942."

Over the years, the MSC has come to be known as a memorial for all Aggie veterans. The MSC hallway displays a plaque for each of the eight Aggie Congressional Medal of Honor winners. Even the grass around the MSC is included in the memorial. Students and visitors are asked not to walk on the MSC grass.

Photo from Texas A&M University Archieves

Statue of Lawrence Sullivan Ross

* Fifty-three live oak trees were planted around Simpson Drill Field to honor the Texas Aggies who sacrificed their lives during World War I. A plaque at the east end of the drill field explains the purpose of the trees.

* The West Gate Memorial is located on the northwest corner of Simpson Drill Field and adjacent to Albritton Tower. The monument commemorates the Aggies killed in World War I.

* The Eli Whiteley Park is named in honor of Eli Whiteley '41 who received the Congressional Medal of Honor for his heroic service in World War II.

* Fish Fountain was given in memory of twelve members of the class of 1938 who gave their lives during World War II.

* The Lawrence Sullivan Ross statue ("Sully") stands on the west side of the Academic Building. Ross was an Indian fighter, Confederate officer, Governor of Texas, and President of Texas A&M. He was truly a "soldier, statesman, and knightly gentleman."

* The Corps Plaza area honors the more than 388 Aggies who have died in wars since World War II.

* The Twelfth Man statue, north of Kyle Field, has a plaque which gives a brief description of the history of Texas A&M's world famous Twelfth Man tradition.

* The Eternal Flame, located at the north entrance to Kyle Field, depicts the undying Aggie Spirit.

"We've Never Been Licked"

A war movie, "We've Never Been Licked," was filmed at
A&M in 1943. It involved a student in the Corps of Cadets who
was posthumously honored at Kyle Field. The film was produced
by Walter Wanger and directed by Jack Rawlins with a script by
Norman Reilly Raine; actors included Richard Quine, Noah
Berry Jr., and Robert Mitchum! The video rights to the film
were obtained by Tom Wisdom, Class of 1960, in 1989. The
class made the video available for purchase and has decided to
donate the profits to Texas A&M and the Corps of Cadets.

The Aggie Ring

Unlike students from other colleges who may choose from many ring designs, all graduates of A&M wear rings of one design. The Ring serves as a common link for former students. When an Aggie sees a Ring on another Aggie's hand, a spontaneous reunion occurs.

The shield on the top of the ring symbolizes our desire to protect the good reputation of our school. The 13 stripes in the shield refer to the 13 original states and symbolize the intense patriotism of graduates of Texas A&M. The five stars in the shield refer to the five phases of development of the student: mind or intellect, body, spiritual attainment, emotional poise, and integrity of character. The eagle is symbolic of agility and power and ability to reach great heights and ambitions.

One side of the ring symbolizes the seal of the State of Texas. The five-pointed star is encircled with a wreath of olive leaves symbolizing achievement and a desire for peace. The liveoak leaves symbolize the strength to fight. They are joined at the bottom by a circled ribbon to show the necessity of joining these two traits to accomplish one's ambitions to serve.

The other side with its ancient cannon, sabre, and rifle symbolizes that Aggies are willing and determined to defend our homeland. The sabre stands for valor and confidence. The rifle and cannon are symbols of preparedness and defense. The crossed flags of the United States and Texas recognize the dual allegiance to nation and state. The gold represents purity and the sacrifices of our parents. Most Aggies feel naked without their ring. I wish I had 10 of them – one for each finger.

Yell Practice

Yell practice is held immediately after supper on designated days to "fire up" the Corps and student body. Midnight Yell is held at midnight prior to each home football game.

Yell practices are led by five students known as Yell Leaders. Three seniors (one, the Head Yell Leader) and two juniors are selected by the student body to serve as the leaders. They lead the yells by using hand signals which are passed through the crowd so everyone knows the right yell. The Yell Leaders also control the crowd and stop unsportsmanlike conduct by using a "rest signal," a single index finger held up. Each member of the Twelfth Man is to keep one eye on the game and one eye on the yell leaders.

The "spirit sessions" are held on the YMCA steps, at the Grove, and on Kyle Field. The band plays, the Yell Leaders lead practice, and "spirit talks" are often given by former students and the Yell Leaders.

After winning a home game, Corps freshmen catch the Yell Leaders and carry them to Prexy's Triangle, throwing them into the fountain, known as the "Fish Pond." If the Aggie team is outscored, the Twelfth Man remains standing in the stadium for a short yell practice to show their continuing support—the 12th Man believes they are the reason the team was outscored. True Aggies never leave a ball game before the final gun sounds. Yell practice is a time set aside to grow as an Aggie.

Hump It

The "hump-it" position involves bending over, knees bent, hands on knees, chins up, and mouths open. This has proven to be the best position to yell loudest.

Thumbs Up

The sign for Aggies is the "Gig 'Em" sign. It is represented by a closed fist with the thumb pointing up. It's the sign of winners.

Fish Camp

The uniqueness of Texas A&M is evident even before a student begins classes. A&M has an orientation program that is second to none in the nation. Fish Camp is one of the institutions that sets A&M apart from other schools. Fish Camp was first instituted at Texas A&M in 1954. The camp is divided into five different four-day sessions and is held at Lakeview Encampment in Palestine, Texas. The purpose is to expose freshman students to the rich heritage and traditions of A&M. Not only do the participants have an opportunity to meet many of the friends that they will have for the rest of their lives, they are also exposed to an array of speakers, counselors, and administrative officials who share valuable hints on study habits, explain how to take tests, tell where students may go for help, and give a briefing on the many organizations which are available to them.

Fish Camp is also a proven training ground for the upper-classmen who serve as camp directors, counselors, and leaders. The Aggie Fish Camp has served as a model camp for other universities throughout the conference and the nation. Fish Camp is another way that Aggies have developed to show students and parents that Aggies truly care about making the transitional period from high school to college as enjoyable and relaxed as possible.

Corps Trips

The Corps attends two out-of-town football games each year. The first Corps Trip was in 1887 when the student body descended on Dallas during the state fair. The trips are taken to show the support of the Twelfth Man. On game day, cadets hold a yell practice, conduct a parade, and then perform as the Twelfth Man as they yell for the team at the game. The Corps and band have to furnish their own transportation and lodging. Corps trips are another way for Aggies to show their love and dedication to Texas A&M.

Reveille

In 1931, some cadets returning from Navasota in a Model-T could not stop when a stray puppy ran onto the road. They picked up the slightly injured pup and brought her to campus. The next morning at reveille, the puppy howled when the bugle call played reveille. She was immediately christened Reveille and became the official mascot of Texas A&M. The first Reveille died on January 18, 1944, after 13 years as mascot. She received a military funeral in the center of Kyle Field. Reveille I and all

Photo from Texas A&M University Archives

Reveille - Our First Lady

succeeding Reveilles are buried at Kyle Field and honored with memorial plaques there. Reveille's privileges on campus include admission to any building and choosing any bunk on which to nap. Aggie fish must speak to her as "Miss Reveille Ma'am." Reveille wears a maroon and white Aggie blanket. Her care is the responsibility of Company E-2.

Silver Taps

This tribute honors deceased Aggie students. Normally, on the first Tuesday of each month, notices are placed at the base of the flagpole in front of the Academic Building. Campus flags are flown at half-mast. The ritual begins around 10:00 p.m. as students gather silently in front of the Academic Building, and friends and family of the deceased stand between the statue of

Silver Taps

Sul Ross and the front steps of the building. All lights are turned out, and passing cars dim their lights for the ceremony.

Music is played by the Albritton Carillon. The Ross Volunteer Firing Squad fires three volleys, and buglers play "Silver Taps" three times from the dome of the Academic Building. Following "Taps," the individuals leave the area silently.

It always seems the wind is blowing. The silence is broken by the "digging-in" of the heels of the R.V. Firing Squad. The cadence is slow and definite. As the 21-gun salute is fired, the resting birds take flight from the trees surrounding the Academic Building. The flapping of their wings seems to pay homage to the deceased. "Taps" is played and we return to our dorms, contemplating life and death and realizing that "but for the grace of God, there go I." Silver Taps is the one tradition I hope you never have to experience. A word to the wise, however — be sure you are prepared! Silver Taps is one of our most sacred traditions and one of the most solemn. It's impossible to forget Silver Taps.

Elephant Walk

The Elephant Walk is an annual event held before the Thanksgiving game. The seniors gather in front of the flagpole on Military Walk and wander aimlessly about, like old elephants about to die. This symbolizes the fact that the seniors will graduate the following spring and will no longer be a part of the Twelfth Man. This, too, is a serious occasion and one which should be respected by all underclassmen, as they, too, will one day no longer be a part of the Twelfth Man.

Aggie Bonfire

Aggie Bonfire

The Aggie Bonfire is the largest in the world and is listed in the Guinness Book of World Records. The Cadets and civilian students prepare for Bonfire throughout the fall semester, cutting wood and setting up the site. Bonfire is made of approximately 9,000 logs that rise 55-100 feet in the air. Around 500 gallons of fuel are used to ignite the logs. Today's Ags, in the spirit of conservation, replant trees in the place of those cut down. Way to go, Ags!

The Head Yell Leader, in the past, and the Redpots, today, coordinate the building of the Bonfire. They raise the funds, choose the cutting site, obtain the needed equipment, communicate with the press, and watch over the construction activities. The two major areas of operation are the cutting area and the stacking area. The students handle the entire operation using several committees.

The Bonfire is held on campus each year before the game with t.u. Bonfire symbolizes two things: the undying flame of love that every Aggie carries in his heart for his school and our burning desire to beat t.u. again. Where else but A&M? Long live Bonfire!

Muster

The Aggie Muster is truly one of the greatest of all Aggie traditions. It is held around the world, wherever Aggies gather each year on April 21, the anniversary of the Texas victory of Sam Houston over Santa Anna's army at San Jacinto. The ceremony honors Texas Aggie students and former students who have died during the year. It is a time for Aggies to renew their pledges of loyalty and friendship to each other and to Texas A&M.

Muster began in 1883. In 1903, the tradition was set for the permanent date of April 21. Muster has been held in European foxholes in World War I, and, during World War II, a ceremony was conducted on Corregidor Island in the Philippines by 25 Aggies led by General George Moore, Class of 1908, in honor of Aggies who had fallen there. That Muster inspired a world-wide Aggie Muster to be held each year.

"Roll Call For The Absent" honors the Aggies who have died during the previous year. A living comrade answers,

Photo from Texas A&M University Archives

Corregidor Muster Reunion (1946)

"Here," for the departed, signifying that the Aggie Spirit continues, and a candle is lit for each such student or former student. The Ross Volunteer Firing Squad fires a 21-gun salute in three volleys and "Silver Taps" is played three times by the buglers.

Hearts and minds are focused on the brevity of life and the

importance of friends as we celebrate the lives of departed Aggies.

Aggie Sports

A&M has been just as successful in producing leaders on the athletic field as it has on and off the battlefield. There's no way to cover all the great Ags, teams, and events, but a few are given to show the variety and quality of Aggie sports.

Aggies have always stressed teamwork, and no single Aggie team has represented that term better than Coach Mark Johnson's 1989 Aggie Baseball Team — the best team in the nation with a 58-7 record. Eleven of the players were drafted into professional baseball. They possessed and represented the best traits in sports — hustle, determination, dedication, unselfishness, spirit, and a never-say-die attitude; time and time again, they would come from behind to win in the last inning. Chuck Knoblauch (1991 American League Rookie of the Year and member of the World Champion Minnesota Twins) was the defensive spark-plug at short-stop, and "Big Bad" John Byington provided the clutch hits. Who will ever forget the Aggie's eight-run outburst in the ninth inning, including Byington's "Grand Slam," which enabled the Ags to overcome a five-run deficit in the first game of a double-header and beat the 'sips. Byington's three-run homer in the last inning of the second game broke a 5-5 tie to seal the win in front of the jubilant Aggie faithful. What a thrill! Just as exciting, was the 1991 three-game sweep of the 'sips at Olsen Field!

Then, there's C.E. "Pat" Olsen '23 who played on the N.Y. Yankees with Babe Ruth and Lou Gehrig. Can you imagine that — WOW! And let's not forget Dave Johnson '64, former Aggie baseball and basketball star, who was the manager of the N.Y.

Mets when they won the 1986 Baseball World Championship.

Aggies have also excelled in track and field events. Polio victim Walter F. "Buddy" Davis '52 overcame all odds and won the Olympic gold medal in the high jump and also played in the NBA. Of course, everyone knows of the track feats and accomplishments of Randy Matson, who won the Olympic Gold in 1968 in the shot put. He was also the first to throw the shot over 70 feet. But did you know he also played basketball at A&M?

Few people know that Coach Paul "Bear" Bryant gave up one of his football scholarships to give Bobby Nichols a golf scholarship. Nichols went on to win the prestigious PGA Championship in 1964.

Then, there is football and the many success stories that program has produced. Topping the list of achievements are the 1939 National Football Championship and the undefeated, unscored-upon teams of 1917 and 1919. But just as sweet were the three consecutive SWC Championships and Cotton Bowl trips in 1985, '86, and '87 under Coach Jackie Sherrill and the 1991 Championship under Coach R.C. Slocum. And, then, there is the famous comeback of 1967 which starred Edd Hargett and Curley Hallman under the direction of Coach Gene Stallings, Class of 1957.

Individual success stories? Well, how about John David Crow? He won the 1957 Heisman Trophy under Coach Bryant. Aggie Steve O'Neal '69 holds the record for the longest punt in NFL history — 98 yards, and, then, there is Tony Franklin '79 who is remembered for kicking 60 yard field goals time and time again — barefoot! Jack Pardee and David Davis are the only Ags to be given scholarships who played six-man football in high school.

Aggie All-Americans include Dave Elmendorf '71, who won All-American honors in baseball and football and was an

Academic All-American in both sports. Kip Corrington '88, also won Academic All-American laurels in football. And the list of Aggie greats doesn't stop there. Great Aggie backs include Routt, Kimbrough, Vick, Woodside, Toney, Wilson, Dickey, Woodard, Todd and Darren Lewis — who owns the all-time SWC rushing crown. And, although he's listed as a quarterback, Bucky Richardson has to be included as one of the most determined Aggie running backs of all time. The renowned Aggie line-backers include names like Simmonini, Roper, Wallace, Ten Napel, Hobbs, and Holland. Defensive backs bring to mind Thomas, Bryant, and Hayes. Linemen include the likes of Childress, Green, Williams, Cheek, Webb, and McCall. Then, there is return man Rod Harris and Aggie "Heart Award" recipient Lance Pavlas. And how about two-sport star Jeff Granger, Greg Hill, Seth Dockery, Rodney Thomas and Sam Adams? Of course our thoughts will always be with James Glenn, Aggie Football Player who died during practice on Kyle

Photo by Kathy Young

Reunion of 1939 National Championship Team

Field in 1991.

Other sports laurels include Coach Shelby Metcalf. He is the only coach in Aggie history to earn his doctoral degree from A&M. And Coach R.C. Slocum who has coached at A&M for close to twenty years. We'll remember names like Beasley and Lenox in basketball; Doug Rau and Wally Moon in baseball; the softball championships; Olympian Linda Cornelius Waltman; and who could ever forget . . . . There's just no end. Throw in the ones you're thinking of and you have the best of the best. We could go on forever! There's just nothing like 'em — Jesus, America, Apple Pie, Hot Dogs, Baseball, and Texas A&M. WHOOP!!!

Chapter 5
False Traditions

MANY PEOPLE try to pull others down to their level. A&M is different. A&M is special. Many are jealous of Aggies and Aggie Spirit. They desire to try to tear A&M down. It is a waste of their time, but they try. Because of that, I wanted to list a few "false traditions" that have no place at A&M. They are not, nor have they ever been, a part of our proud heritage. If it's not uplifting and positive, then it's not an Aggie tradition. For example:

👎 It is not a tradition that if Bonfire falls before midnight, Aggies will be out-scored. Wrong! Totally false! Also, while we're on the subject of Bonfire, I might as well take this opportunity to elaborate on my feelings about this topic that is so dear to the hearts of all Aggies.

It saddens me that A&M has a number of faculty members who have nothing better to do than sign a petition to outlaw Bonfire. To call the Bonfire "a needless waste and a source of embarrassment" for A&M causes one to wonder about the wisdom and foresight of these scholarly professors. For these men and women of reputation to make statements that are based on untruth, incorrect data, and cloudy ideas of this magnitude boggles the mind.

Possibly, many of these professors have never had to work in the "real world" and have only been confined to the classroom or research labs of the "academic world." If so, maybe they would be happier to expound their theories at t.u. or Rice. I am sure some of their liberal philosophies are too far from immediate reality and, therefore, they are unable to understand that the valuable, useful, and lasting values of cooperation, communication, organization, leadership, hard work, and accomplishment gained through an adventure such as building the Bonfire are very useful and needed tools in the "work world."

To say Bonfire should be done away with because the students who work on the Bonfire go to sleep in class and miss the lectures of these professors is also invalid. Oh, I am sure many students do go to sleep in class. After all, there is a lot of hard work, dedication, lost sleep, and missed meals. However, if memory serves me correctly and if the word that comes to me now from many present-day Aggies is true, students go to sleep in class when professors are dull and boring. When professors are more interested in their research and in writing a book for their inflated egos than they are in teaching, their classes will normally be dull and boring. I admire anyone for taking a stand, but at least take a stand for some issue that needs to be addressed — like drunk driving, drinking at Bonfire, or date rape. Surely these dissenters know these issues are a little more vital and destructive than the cutting down of a few trees once a year. Perhaps they could protest the number and the high cost of books that are required for their courses. But to make a protest of this nature in the name of conservation, while driving around in gas-guzzling cars that pollute the environment and deplete the oil supply, is weak and pathetic. I, too, am very concerned about our environment, but let's be real. Many forestry experts encourage controlled burning of some forest areas. This allows for new growth and reforestation. Many land-owners want their land cleared of timber in order to plant grass or other types of trees. I will say and admit that when I was at A&M and had the privilege of helping to build four Aggie Bonfires, we did not replant trees in the place of those we cut down. I am sorry for that and regret that we did not. It was out of ignorance on our part. We just did not know. That is why I am so pleased that the Aggies of today do replant trees in the place of those they cut down. What a great new Aggie tradition.

Yes, it is true that an Aggie's love for his school can be expressed in other ways. And it is — in ways that no other school can duplicate. The Bonfire, however, is one of those ways. So, if those who want to stop Bonfire are truly concerned about destroying the environment, a good way to prove it is to drive a non-ozone-destroying, horse-drawn buggy to the cutting area and plant a tree for every one that is cut down. I am sure the Yell Leaders and Red Pots will be appreciative of the assistance. Long live Bonfire! Long live the planting of trees! And long live the vast majority of the professors and administrators of Texas A&M who understand, appreciate, support, and love the many unique and time-honored traditions of Aggieland.

 It is not a tradition to tell filthy jokes at Midnight Yell Practice. Filthy jokes are not fables. They are not macho.

They are wrong and everyone knows it. Aggies don't have
to try to impress anyone. Aggies know what is in good taste;
just do what's right! A&M is special; it's up to you to keep
it that way.

👎 It is not a tradition to copy any antic of any other school. For
instance, to chant, "poor teasips!" is not in keeping with
Aggie Spirit.

👎 It is not a tradition to be drunk at Yell Practice or anywhere
else. Aggies have more sense than that. Let's prove it! The
point is not if you've ever seen an Aggie who's had too much
to drink; the point is that it is not tradition. Being in any
condition other than sober does not uplift the true image of
an Aggie. Old fashioned or not, it's still the truth.

👎 It is not a tradition for Aggie fans to throw anything at any
ball game. Teasips are great at this. Let them be best at
something.

👎 It is not a tradition to yell *against* other teams. Just yell *for*
the Aggies. (Exception: it is always permissible to yell
against t.u.) However, Aggies are always only *for* A&M.

👎 It is not an original tradition to sing only the second verse
of the "Aggie War Hymn." The "War Hymn" was written
by Mr. J. V. Wilson in the midst of battle during World War
I. I am sure this maroon-blooded Aggie did not intend for
the first verse to be ignored. Mr. Bob Boone, director of
"The Singing Cadets" for more than 25 years, has advocated
the singing of both verses for years. With a little effort, we
could learn the first verse, and, then, we would be able to

sing both verses as intended. To do so would truly be going back to the original tradition. Let's do it! Bite the bullet! Take a stand! The first verse (see Chapter 6) speaks more of A&M anyway. Try it, you'll like it.

It is not a tradition for A&M students to wear the logo of any other school on their shirts or jackets on the A&M campus. This holds true for the civilian students as well as the corps students. An Aggie's dedication, time, money, and devotion are to A&M. It's only been in recent years that students started wearing the A&M logo on any color shirt other than maroon. Some of us old Ags aren't even happy about that — but, at least, it's not the logo of some other school.

It is not a tradition to have other functions going on at the same time as an Aggie sporting event. Parties are to be held after the game is over. Anyone (most anyone) can enroll at A&M as a student. There is, however, a big difference in being a student and being an Aggie. There is no room for two percenters at A&M.

It is not a tradition for Elephant Walk to be a circus or a time of disrespect. Seniors are to walk about the campus in a somber mood formed up in a single line. It is not a time for joking and laughing. It is a time for reflection over the events and memories of the past which will soon be no more.

It is not a tradition for only the Corps and a few civilian students to say, "Howdy!" All Aggie students are to say, "Howdy!" to each other and to all visitors on campus. A&M is nationally known for having a friendly campus. Let's keep it that way. It's not that tough to do. Those that have any problem with this should look elsewhere to further their education. When you sign up to go to A&M, you sign up to be more than a student — you sign up to be an Aggie, and that means getting involved.

It is not a tradition for an Aggie athlete or student to "hot dog" or to perform any other antic which draws attention to an individual rather than the whole team. We are known for having more class than any other school. We are known for being original. We don't have to copy any other team or school in any other way.

Chapter 6

Aggie Compositions

Songs, Poems, Yells and Sayings

EVERYTHING ABOUT A&M is special and unique. Our songs, poems, yells, and sayings are all from the heart. They are more than words set to rhyme — they are feelings; they are real; they are from the depths of our spirit.

SONGS

The Spirit of Aggieland

> Some may boast of prowess bold,
> Of the schools they think so grand,
> But there's a spirit can ne'er be told,
> It's the spirit of Aggieland.
> **(Second Verse)**
> 'Tho from Alma Mater so far I roam,

My whole heart shall be with you e'er;
I'll always be proud to call you my own,
It's the Aggieland so fair.
(Chorus After Each Verse)
We are the Aggies - the Aggies are we,
True to each other as Aggies can be.
We've got to FIGHT boys,
We've got to fight!
We've got to fight for Maroon and White.
After they've boosted all the rest,
They will come and join the best,
For we are the Aggies - the Aggies are we.
We're from Texas AMC.
(Second Chorus - Second time Only)
T-E-X-A-S A-G-G-I-E,;
Fight! Fight! Fight-fight-fight!
Fight! Maroon! White-white-white!
A-G-G-I-E,
Texas! Texas! A-M-C!
Gig'em, Aggies! 1! 2! 3!
Farmers fight! Farmers fight!
Farmers, farmers fight!

Words by Marvin H. Mimms
Music by Richard J. Dunn

The Aggie War Hymn

Hullabaloo, Caneck! Caneck!
Hullabaloo, Caneck! Caneck!
All Hail! to dear old Texas A and M.
Rally around Maroon and White;
Good luck to the dear old Texas Aggies,
They are the boys who show the real old Fight.

That good old Aggie spirit thrills us
And makes us yell and yell and yell;
So let's fight for dear old Texas A and M.
We're going to beat you all to
Chig-ga-roo-gar-em!
Chig-ga-roo-gar-em!
Rough! Tough!
Real stuff! Texas A&M.
Goodbye to Texas University,
So long to the Orange and White.
Good Luck to dear old Texas Aggies,
They are the boys that show the real old fight.
"The eyes of Texas are upon you..."
That is the song they sing so well?
So good-bye to Texas University,
We're going to beat you all to
Chig-ga-roo-gar-em!
Chig-ga-roo-gar-em!
Rough! Tough!
Real stuff! Texas A&M.

Words and Music by J.V. "Pinky" Wilson

The Twelfth Man

Texas Aggies down in Aggieland
We've got Aggie spirit to a man!
Stand united! That's the Aggie theme.
We're the twelfth man on the team,
When we're down, the goin's rough and tough
We just grin and yell we've got the stuff
To fight together for the Aggie dream,
We're the twelfth man on that
FIGHTIN' AGGIE TEAM!

Written by Lil Munnerlyn

YELLS

Aggies copy no one. Even our Yells are unique.

Gig'em Aggies

Yeaaaaaa, gig'em Aggies!

Aggies

A-G-G-I-E-S
A-G-G-I-E-S
Yeaaaa, Fight 'em, Aggies!

Farmers Fight

Farmers Fight! Farmers Fight!
Fight-Fight
Farmers, Farmers, Fight!

Military

Squads left! Squads right!
Farmers, Farmers, we're all right
Load, ready, aim, fire, BOOM!
A&M! Give us room!

Old Army

A-a-a-a R-r-r- M-m-m
Y-y-y, (drop voice)
T-t-t-t-t A-a-a M-m-m
C-c-c (drop voice)
Yea-a-a! Old Army Fight!

Kyle Field

K-Y-L-E F-I-E-L-D
Yeaaaaaaaa, Kyle Field!
Fight'em, Aggies!

Fifteen for Team

Rah! Rah! Rah! Team!
A-a-a-a
R-r-r-r
M-m-m-m
Y-y-y-y
Yea Army! Fight 'em!

Horse Laugh

Riffety! Riffety! Riff-Raff!
Chiffety! Chiffety! Chiff-Chaff!
Riff-Raff! Chiff-Chaff!
Let's give'em the horse laugh!
Ha-a-a-a-a-a

POEMS

There are many poems that express our love for A&M and
its traditions. Here are a few.

The Last Corps Trip

It was Judgment Day in Aggieland
        and tenseness filled the air;
All knew there was a trip at hand,
        but not a soul knew where.

Assembled on the drill field
        was the world-renowned Twelfth Man;
the entire fighting Aggie Team
        and the famous AggieBand.

And out in front with Royal Guard
        the reviewing party stood;
Saint Peter and his angel staff
        were choosing bad from good.

First he surveyed the Aggie Team
        and in terms of an angel swore,
"By Jove, I do believe I've seen
        this gallant group before.

"I've seen them play since way back when,
        and they've always had the grit;
I've seen 'em lose and I've seen 'em win,
        but I've never seen 'em quit.

"No need for us to tarry here
        deciding upon their fates;
'Tis as plain as the halo on my head
        that they've opened Heaven's gates."

And when the Twelfth Man heard this,
        they let out a mighty yell
that echoed clear to Heaven
        and shook the gates of Hell.

"And what group is this upon the side?"
        Saint Peter asked his aide,

"That swelled as if to burst with pride
    when we our judgment made?"

"Why, sir, that's the Cadet Corps
    that's known both far and wide;
For backing up their fighting team
    whether they won or lost or tied."

"Well, then," said Saint Peter,
    "It's very plain to me;
That within the realms of Heaven
    they should spend eternity.

"And have the Texas Aggie Band
    at once begin to play;
for their fates, too, we must decide
    upon this crucial day."

And the drum major so hearing
    slowly raised his hand;
And said, "Boys, let's play the Spirit
    for the last time in Aggieland."

And the band poured forth the anthem
    in notes both bright and clear;
And ten thousand Aggie voices
    sung the song they hold so dear.

And when the band had finished,
    Saint Peter wiped his eyes
And said, "It's not so hard to see
    they're meant for Paradise."

And the colonel of the Cadet Corps said,
    as he stiffly took his stand,
"It's just another Corps trip, boys,
     We'll all march in behind the band."
                    — *Philo H. DuVal, Jr. '51*

Dan Debenport '91, a Buck Weirus Spirit Award winner, wrote the following poem about his first Aggie Muster while a freshman at A&M. Dan now serves his country as a Marine officer, but his eternal love for A&M and his Aggie buddies is clearly depicted in this poem.

First Muster

Tonight was Aggie Muster, my first one as an Ag.
Although my legs were sore, I didn't seem to drag.
I stood beside Brant and Mark, my buddies 'till the end.
We started as strangers, but now we're best of friends.
I realized what Muster means, as I heard the roll being called,
and I know I'm just a fish, but my stay here will seem small.
For me it was unique, I stood by an honored guest;
her name is Reveille V, and for mascots she's the best.
As I watched the candles light, I felt that Aggie pride —
like the eternal flame glowing, my heart burned deep inside.
I know my buds and I will someday all part way,
But on April 21, our souls will never stray.
                    — *Dan Debenport '91*

Cliff Dugosh '86, another recipient of the Buck Weirus Spirit Award, wrote the poems that follow. You will sense his true Aggie Spirit as you read them.

A Season of Memories
(The Aggie Baseball Team of '89)

The season of a lifetime
    has now come to an end;
you've left your mark for years to come
    with seven losses and fifty-eight wins.

You've rounded those last few bases
    with loud resounding cheers;
in the eyes of people everywhere
    you'll be heroes throughout the years.

The ball is thrown, the ball is hit
    the crowd is on its feet;
kids see you as their idols
    not once did you retreat.

Life is made of memories
    and this season there's been plenty;
teamwork, closeness and brotherhood
    stand out among the many.

The integrity of character
    and times you came from behind,
are the *true* marks of a champion
    that stand out in everyone's mind.

As you round the bases in the game of life
    may God be with you as you go;
you'll always be thought of as heroes –
    ones that we were all so glad to know.

—Cliff Dugosh '86

A Special Place

You often hear of a special place
    that people think so grand;
the one we all hold so dear
    we call it Aggieland.

Here you find many special ways
    and people who really care;
it's a place filled with tradition
    you'll find it everywhere.

Out on Duncan Field
    is a sight that'll never tire;
since 1909, we've gathered the wood
    to show our burning desire.

Muster, on April 21st
    is the only place to be;
we've gathered each and every year
    since 1883.

We call the names of the ones we knew
    the Aggies here no more;
we answer the "Roll" and shed a tear
    while their spirit's forever more.

The emotions felt at Silver Taps
    when the Bugle's blow so clear,
are the memories that will never fade–
    the ones we hold so dear.

But what it is that makes this place
    such a special one to me,
are the people we meet and the friends we make
    they'll last an eternity.

You'll find your life is greatly enhanced
    by those you meet wherever you go,
you are made up of bits and pieces
    of every person you come to know.

So take these bits and pieces with you
    wherever you call home,
and this special place will be with you always
    no matter where you roam.

                              —Cliff Dugosh '86

That Glorious April Day

There's a long maroon unbroken line
    that always marches on,
it brings us all together
    and makes our hearts so strong.

We've gathered each and every year
    since 1883;
Muster, on April 21st
    is the only place to be.

Once a year we call the names
    of the ones we knew so well;
yes one day too, we will be called
    when - time will tell.

The reverence shown at Muster
    the gleam of the candle light,
are the memories always cherished
    of that April 21st night.

Here, deep emotions are always felt
    about this school so grand,
and about the ones who've gone before us
    to the promised land.

And for this friend that went before
    spreading a little cheer,
on that glorious April day
    someone will answer "Here".

We unite on this day, a reunion for all
    as honor fills the air;
we renew old friendships and remember times past
    and it shows how much we care.

The feelings felt at Muster
    those that never will depart,
are invisible to the naked eye
    and felt only with the heart.

                             —Cliff Dugosh '86

The Boys In White

Back at the College of A&M
    during days that have come and gone,
tradition started that has remained unchanged
    one that will always march on.

It's a tradition full of honor
        where spirit comes from the heart;
many things make this school
        unique this one sets it apart.

There are five guys to represent us
        in everything that we do,
they're called the Aggie Yell Leaders and
        they're among the proud, select few.

They lead the yells while wearing white
        and keep the spirit going strong;
their blood runs a deep maroon
        as they pass our heritage along.

As a Yell Leader all eyes are upon you
        by people everywhere;
you're now representing all of A&M
        show us you really care.

Your actions on the field
        as in life speak louder than words,
so do your best, keep your head up high
        and your message will always be heard.

You represent thousands that have gone before
        and thousands yet to come;
it's an awesome responsibility
        and a heck of a lot of fun.

Realize your moves that lie ahead
        unnoticed they will never go,

to many you are Texas A&M
    you represent a first-class show.

All that's asked is that you do your best
    in everything for which you strive,
that's the true sign of an Aggie
    the integrity that rules our life.

For the five known as the Yell Leaders
    always give all of your heart's desire,
and as you lead the Aggie Spirit
    you'll set our souls on fire.

—Cliff Dugosh '86

SAYINGS

These are just a few of the many.

👍 I would rather flunk out of A&M than graduate with honors from t.u.

👍 If t.u. were playing the University of Moscow in Red Square, I would be on the goal post waving a big red flag.

👍 West Point is a good prep school for A&M.

👍 t.u., t.u. — where the girls are girls and the boys are too.

👍 I would rather go 0-11 and be an Aggie than be National Champs and be a 'sip.

👍 Texan by birth, Aggie by the grace of God.

👍 Aggies may get out-scored, but they never lose.

👍 We've never been licked.

👍 I would rather eat barbed wire than go to t.u.

👍 If I had a low IQ, I would go to t.u., too.

👍 Shoulders back and heads up high, the Corps of Cadets is passing by.

👍 Aggies feed the world.

👍 No Aggie was without a job during the Great Depression.

👍 BOSS — What you call an Aggie five years after he graduates.

👍 "Howdy!", "Gig'em!", "Farmer's Fight!", "'Ol Army!"

👍 The 4 responses allowed by a fish:
1. "Yes, sir!"
2. "No, sir!"
3. "No excuse, sir!"
4. "Sir, not being informed to the highest degree of accuracy, I hesitate to articulate for fear I may deviate from the true course of rectitude. In short, sir, I am a very dumb fish and do not know, sir."

👍 Highway 6 runs both ways (so does Amtrak for you new Ags).

👍 Love it or leave it.

👍 Hullabaloo!

Chapter 7

Aggie Slanguage

AGGIES HAVE a language that is unique. The following is a part of that language:

AGGIE: You & me; one of us; derived from the first letters in agricultural. A student of Texas A&M University.

AGGIELAND: Home of Texas A&M University.

AIR CRAPPER: A member of the Corps who is in an Air Force outfit.

ASSOCIATION OF FORMER STUDENTS: There is no such thing at A&M as an alumni association or Ex-Aggie; there are only former students. You do not have to graduate from A&M to be a member. Once an Aggie, always an Aggie!

BAG MONSTER: The force that breaks down your will power and pulls you back to bed even though you need to study.

It usually strikes hardest during finals week.

BAG RAT: A student who loses a fight with the Bag Monster. This happens a lot.

BATT: The campus newspaper, THE BATTALION.

BIRD DOG: The third party of "three's a crowd."

BONFIRE: The world's largest bonfire, which is burned before the t.u. game.

B.Q.: Member of the Aggie Band.

BULL: Superfluous conversation or a military officer.

BULL RING: Disciplinary drill for the purpose of removing demerits.

BULL SESSION: Talk fest.

C.O.: Commanding Officer.

CORPS HAPPY: Obsessed with the Corps.

C.Q.: Call to quarters. Charge of quarters.

CRAPPED OUT: Being either mentally, physically, or emotionally exhausted.

CRUNCHIE: A member of the Corps in an Army outfit.

C.T.: Any member of the Corps of Cadets.

DAY DUCK: A student living off campus.

D&C: Junior or senior in the Corps who does not have a contract with one of the military services.

DEAN'S TEAM: List of students passing less than 12 hours work.

D.M.S.: Distinguished military student.

EAST GATE: Main entrance to the College.

FISH: Any freshman student.

FLUSHED: When an A&M student gets a "Dear John" or "Dear Mary" letter, as the case may be, from his or her sweetee. It is an unwritten tradition that an Aggie gets at least one flush letter their freshman year.

FRAT RAT: Male student at Cookie Pusher school who is a member of a fraternity.

GRASS: It is a senior privilege in the Corps to walk on the grass. Exceptions to this rule exist in that nobody is supposed to walk on the grass around the MSC or across from the Corps area since these are both memorials.

GROUND POUNDER: Army Cadet.

GUNG HO: Being enthusiastic about the Corps, its traditions, and love for A&M.

HANDLE: Title. "fish" or "Mister" used before name.

"HIGHWAY SIX RUNS BOTH WAYS": A phrase meaning that if you are unhappy with any aspect of Aggie life, you are free to leave. An equivalent phrase is "Texas A&M — love it or leave it."

HOLE: Aggie's room. Four walls, table, chair, and bed.

HORIZONTAL ENGINEERING: Napping.

HOWDY!: Traditional Aggie greeting.

KAMPUS KOPS: Members of the university police force.

LATE LIGHTS: Midnight oil; privilege of lights after taps.

LEATHER LEGS: Senior cadet.

MEAL HOUND: Aggie who takes food from tables other than his own, a freshman privilege.

MILITARY WALK: Ancient street of the old area running from Sbisa to Rudder Tower. The street has been converted into a pedestrian walk.

NON-REG: Non-regulation. Civilian students.

NORTH GATE: Area across the street from the main post office on University Drive.

O.D.: Officer of the Day; olive drab (color of army uniforms).

OL' ARMY: Corps of Cadets (Like it "used to be").

OLD LADY: One who shares your money, shaving cream, toothpaste, etc.; the roommate.

ONE-WAY CORPS TRIP: Permanent trip home at the dean's request; scholastic dismissal.

PARENT'S WEEKEND: An activity set aside to honor Aggie parents, usually in the spring. It is also the day when awards are presented. Parents of the Year are named at this time.

POOP: General term meaning "information." Something really exciting is referred to as "hot poop."

POT: Helmet liner.

PREXY: The president of Texas A&M University.

PREXY'S MOON: Light on the dome of the Academic Building.

PRIVILEGE: Something achieved by virtue of rank.

RAMS: Demerits.

REST: Be quiet!

R.H.I.P.: Rank hath its privileges.

R.H.I.R.: Rank hath its responsibilities.

ROSS VOLUNTEERS: Military society named for Lawrence Sullivan Ross. Also known as "R.V.'s."

SACK OUT: Engage in horizontal engineering.

SENIOR BOOTS: Brown boots worn only by seniors in the Corps.

SHOOT THE BULL: Talk.

SHORT STOP: Take food before upperclassman.

SIGN IN: To report to guard room at specified times; used as punishment.

SUGAR REPORT: Sweet letter from the girl friend.

SULLY: Statue of Lawrence Sullivan Ross, former governor of Texas and former president of A&M. It stands in front of the Academic Building.

SURGE BUTT: Junior in the Corps, identified by white braid on his cap.

TEASIPPER: Students from t.u. Sometimes shortened to 'sip.

TEXSUSS AEH & EHM UUNIVERHSITEEIE: Popular pronunciation of Texas A&M.

TOP-KICK: First Sergeant.

TRIGON: Military Science Building; where the Bulls (military officers) work and govern the Corps.

t.u.: Aggie term for The University of Texas, that small secular (Berkeley Of The South) school in central Texas. The only word a fish can abbreviate.

TWO PERCENTERS: The 2% of the students who do not display true Aggie Spirit.

WEST GATE: Old entrance to the campus (near the railroad).

WHIPPING OUT: Meeting other Aggies with a handshake and a "howdy." Also means to ace a quiz or do a spectacular job on anything.

WILD CAT: Yell of approval.

ZIP: Senior in the Corps, identified by gold braid on his hat, senior boots, and a noticeable strut.

AGGIE SLANGUAGE USED IN THE MESS HALLS

No wonder we were always hungry — we didn't know what to ask for the first three weeks. If you're like me, maybe you've forgotten some of the terms we used for our mess hall slanguage. Hopefully, the following list will refresh the memory of former students and will also be a valuable source of information for future and present Ags.

ARTILLERY: Beans
BABY: Mustard
BLANKETS: Hot-cakes
BLOOD: Catsup
BULL NECK: Meat
CACKLE: Eggs

COW: Milk
CUSH: Dessert
DEAL: Bread
DIRT: Black pepper
DOPE: Coffee
DRY-CUSH: Cookies
GREASE: Butter
GUN WADDING: Jelly fritters
HORSE FEED: Corn
LUBE: Gravy
MUD: Chocolate milk or cocoa.
MUSH: Hot cooked cereal
POPEYE: Spinach
RABBIT: Salad
RED RABBIT: Beets and tomatoes
REG: Syrup
SAWDUST: Sugar
SCABS: Flaky cereal
SHINGLES: Crackers
SHOT: Peas
SHOTGUN: Pepper sauce
SHOVEL: Spoon
SKY: Water
SOUR: Lemon
SOUR RABBIT: Pickles and onions
SPUDS: Potatoes
STUD: Tea
SUNSHINE: Carrots or carrots and peas
SWEETSTUFF: Jelly or preserves
TIMBER: Toothpicks
WILDCAT: Pineapple
WINCHESTER: Worcestershire sauce
WORMS: Spaghetti

Chapter 8

My Favorite Aggie Stories

"WELLLLL, OOOOOLLLL' ARMMMYYY!!"

GOT A little story for you Ags. They're hard to believe – but they're all true! I know. I was there.

Hot Peppers

Background:

Aggies are expected not only to meet and greet everyone with whom they come into contact, but also to remember their names. This is especially true for fish (freshmen). For sure, a fish must know everyone in the dorm and outfit, their class, their hometown, and their major. One of the worst mistakes a fish can make is to call someone by the wrong name; topping that is to call them the name of a lowerclassman. In other words, it would be less than advisable for a fish to call a senior by a junior's or, heaven forbid, a sophomore's name.

Story:

Mid-way through our fish year (long past the time given fish to know all members of their outfit), fish Herb Pounds from Gonzales was walking down the darkened halls of Dorm 6 to visit me. Just before he reached my room, he heard someone down the hall behind him. He "hit the wall" (stood at attention against the hall wall), and tried to see who it was so he could speak to him. It was Mr. Frausto, a junior in our outfit, but because of the distance and darkness, fish Pounds could not identify who he was.

Taking a chance, Pounds said, "Howdy, Mr. Rovello, sir." (Rovello was a Sophomore in our outfit). Of course, Frausto was beside himself and directed fish Pounds to come to his (Frausto's) room. As fish Pounds drew closer, he, of course, could tell that it was Frausto instead of Rovello. However, Pounds did not want to "give in" at this point, so he continued to "play dumb" (which wasn't hard) and acted like he couldn't remember Mr. Frausto's name.

After Frausto chewed out Pounds, he gave him a couple of hot peppers to eat. Then, he asked again, "fish Pounds, what is my name?"

This time fish Pounds called him, "Mr. Gonzales, sir!" (another sophomore). This, of course, led to more "chewing out" and five more peppers to eat.

Again the question, "fish Pounds, what is my name?"

The reply, "Mr. Biggs, sir." Biggs was another sophomore. Insert a few more hot peppers to chew.

Exasperated, Frausto asked again, "What is my name, fish Pounds?"

Pounds, with the expression that only he could get on his face, "went the distance" this time with his reply, "fish Cox!" Well, that did it. Pounds had just called our junior scholastic officer a fish. Frausto made Pounds eat the whole bottle of hot peppers. (There is more to the story, but you can probably guess the outcome.)

Burning Bibs

Background:

Eating in the mess hall was one of the most dreaded events for a fish. You go there to (1) listen to announcements, (2) give meal-service to upperclassmen, (3) run hot-corner (insuring hot food is on the table), and (4) eat, if you have time. It was a time for many questions regarding A&M, the campus, and other trivia to be thrust upon the fish. Freshmen wore their napkins tucked in their shirts; upperclassmen laid theirs on their laps. Most tables had two fish on the end closest to the aisle, two more fish in the middle, a couple of sophomores and a junior and senior. A freshman's only friends were other freshmen class-mates. Fish always stand up for their "fish buddies."

To "get back" at an upperclassman was the ultimate goal of every fish and a source of a great sense of victory. Often, seniors would direct a fish to pull some "good bull" on some other senior buddy, but it was still scary for the fish. All fish were required to carry matches in their pockets at all times. This was in case a senior would tell a fish to "burn someone's bib." Normally, when told to burn a bib, the fish would crawl on all fours down the aisle to the end of the victims table, which had his two fish buddies there. Then, he would proceed down under the middle of the table until the victim was reached. Once there, the match would be lit and the bib would be set on fire. The fish would immediately retreat, still on all- fours, to his own table. The victim would pour water on his bib (and, of course, his uniform), jump to his feet, and look for the perpetrator of the crime — usually to no avail.

Story:

After a while, we fish would become quite expert in performing this clandestine operation and would get a little daring in our willingness to take risks. On one such occasion, when told to burn the bib of one of my not-so-favorite upperclassmen, I decided to remain under the table after the "burning" rather than crawling off at a fast pace. It worked! As usual, the victim jumped to his feet, looking everywhere (except under his table) for me. After he sat back down to continue his meal, I removed the bib from my shirt and carefully placed it across the victim's lap. I lit this second bib and, thankfully, had the good sense to crawl away this time. I and my fish buddies rejoiced in our victory and "pay-back."

Two Feet Of Twine

Background:

Same as that described in "Burning Bibs" with the exception that instead of burning the bib of the victim, the goal is to tie the leg of the victim to his chair.

Story:

I sat at the mess hall table of my Squadron's Commanding Officer, Mr. Don Thompson, sir, from Luling. It was during the first week of our fish year. (I was still scared, to say the least.) Mr. Thompson said, "fish Cox, I want you to start carrying two feet of twine with you in your pocket."

My response, of course, was, "Yes, sir." I didn't know why he wanted me to do it, but I wouldn't dare ask why. After chow, I went to the dorm and cut off exactly two feet of twine — *exactly* two feet. I carried it with me everywhere I went.

Finally, some three weeks later during chow, Mr. Thompson asked me if I had the twine. Expecting an award or something good for complying with his directions, I proudly replied, "Yes, sir." My excitement vanished quickly, however, because his next directive was to take the twine and tie Mr. Daugherty's leg to his chair. Mr. Daugherty was a senior going into the Marines, and we called him "Jungle Jim." I never saw him smile, and I was sure he had no conscience. Keep in mind, this was the first time any of us had been asked to carry out an assignment of this nature.

Well, being the "good fish," I started my crawl to Mr. Daugherty. I went under at my fish buddies' end of the table and made it to Mr. Daugherty. I nervously wrapped the twine around his leg and the leg of his chair and was trying to tie a knot with two shaking hands while crouched on my knees. All of a sudden, the chairs moved back from the table. I was crouched under it like a trapped rat. Mr. Daugherty reached under the table, grabbed me by my shirt lapels, and dragged me out into the aisle. I was still on my knees — not because I was begging for mercy but because my legs were too weak to stand. About that time, he yanked me up and held me about three inches off the ground with my nose about three inches from his. I was stiff at attention. He must have thought I was deaf because he spoke to me as if I were on the other side of the mess hall.

After several minutes of lecture, Mr. Thompson came to my rescue by calling me back to my chair and table to finish my meal. As fate would have it, we had soup for supper that night. By the time my spoon reached my lips, all of the soup had vibrated out due to the shaking of my entire body. My thoughts again turned to New Boston, home, and to "where is my mother?" What a night!

Five Buttons

Background:

It is of utmost importance for an Aggie to dress sharply. All buttons must be buttoned, gig-line must be straight, and all cables (threads) must be removed. It is the responsibility of "Wet-Heads" to insure that the fish are properly attired. If found to be wanton in this area, a fish is *severely* ridiculed and chastised for such gross ineptness.

Story:

I was found to be "wanton" one day during our daily inspection prior to marching to chow. I had left one button unbuttoned on my shirt. After being reprimanded at some length for my utter negligence, wet-head Mr. C (name withheld to protect the guilty) directed me to come to his room after chow to receive further and more detailed instructions and training in the proper dress of a future military officer.

After dragging out the eating of my meal for as long as I could, I finally reported to his room as instructed. Once there, thirty additional minutes were used by Mr. C to expound upon his expertise, skills, knowledge, and ability in the area of proper apparel. When he finally completed his dissertation, he was ready to teach me a lesson which would be indelibly etched in my mind to the degree that I would never leave a button unbuttoned again for the rest of my life; he was going to cut the button off my shirt and make me sew it back on. (I, of course, had been standing at rigid attention for more than 30 minutes by now.)

He was so proud of himself and the ingenious way he had found to teach me a lesson. The only problem was that he couldn't find a knife or pair of scissors in his room to use to remove my button. After stumbling around looking for some time, in exasperation, he finally asked me if I had a knife in my pocket that he could use. (Of all the nerve — he wanted me to give him my knife so he could cut off my button so that I would have to sew it back on my shirt. Really now.) Of course, I told him I didn't have a knife. He told me to wait in his room at attention against the wall while he went next door to borrow a knife. I, of course, replied. "Yes, Sir."

When he left the room, I immediately pulled out my ol' trusty Buck knife and cut off five buttons from his shirt in his closet. My only regret is that I cut them all off the same shirt. I should have cut one off each of his five shirts. (Hey, don't hiss; I was only a fish.)

When Mr. C returned to the room, he cut off one of my buttons and smugly said, "Well, that's the way it goes, fish Cox!" I said, "Yes, sir, that's the way it goes, sir." He never found out how it happened, and I'm in hopes that he is not reading this right now.

•Trick Or Treat

Background:

Seniors usually make the fish go "trick or treating" for them during Halloween. Talk about embarrassing. I mean, for 18-year-old college students to walk up to a house alongside an 8-year-old was demeaning. But seniors were also known to make fish go "trick or treat" for dessert from other upperclassmen in the dining halls (mess halls). (Refer to "Burning Bibs" and "Two Feet of Twine" stories for additional background.)

Story:

My commanding officer, Mr. Thompson, told me to "trick or treat" for Mr. Daugherty's cush (dessert). That's right, ol "Jungle Jim" himself. Standing at the end of the table at attention, I bellowed, "Trick or Treat, Mr. Daugherty, sir!"

Slowly glancing upward, while shaking his head in disbelief, he asked, "Did you say, `Trick or Treat,' fish Cox?"

"Yes, sir," I replied. (By this time I was much braver than I was when I tried to tie his leg to the chair.)

"And just what is it you want, fish Cox?" I looked around and saw the "cush" for the night was "cold cow" (Dixie cups of vanilla ice cream). I decided it would be good bull to get each of the upperclassmen's cold cow (but leaving my fish buddies their cush), so I said, "All of the upperclassmen's cold cow, sir!" (I was going to share it with my other fish buddies.)

"All of it?" he asked.

"Yes, sir, all of it," I confirmed, undeterred.

So, he gathered up all of the upperclassmen's cold cow from his table and the table next to him. It was a haul — eight, at least! "Wow, I'll be a hero!" I thought to myself as I gathered them up in my arms and began to retreat to my table. "Whoa, fish Cox. Where are you going?" Mr. Daugherty asked.

"To my table, Mr. Daugherty, sir," I replied.

"Not until you've eaten your `treat' fish Cox. Have a seat here beside me and get started." EIGHT DIXIE CUPS of M-E-L-T-I-N-G VANILLA ICE CREAM. I'd take a bite and a swallow of water, a bite and a swallow . . . . Needless to say, to this very day, I still have trouble eating vanilla ice cream.

The Vacuum De-cleaner

Background:

One of our fish buddies had an upperclassman friend in another dorm who had a vacuum cleaner. He had not changed bags all semester, and it was close to the end of the semester. To say the least, the bag was full.

Story:

One of our not-so-popular "wet-heads" had been especially hard on us fish for the entire week. (His girl friend must have "flushed" him.) Anyway, we were able to get into his room one day while he was in class and thought we'd do him the favor of vacuuming his room — well, sort of.

We reversed the vacuum, expecting all of the dirt in the bag to be dumped on the floor in one large pile. To our surprise, dust immediately filled the entire room, from corner to corner, and from floor to ceiling. We couldn't move at first; we just stood there in disbelief. We finally looked at each other, died laughing, and quickly excused ourselves from the room and the dorm. Thankfully, we were smart enough by this time of the year to remove all of the dust from our clothes, shoes, and body. REVENGE! Oh, how sweet it was. We never got caught.

17 Pair Of Boots To Shine

Background:

Training received through the Corps is an integral part of a cadet's life. Many times, the benefits of such training (some call it hazing) is not readily observable to the recipient — especially when the recipient is a fish.

My son, John Blair '95, and my daughter, Cristy Cay '98, have always marveled at my expertise in shining their Roper boots to where, as they say, "They look like new, Dad!" I'm not so sure they really mean it, or if that's just their subtle way of getting ol' Dad to do their shining for them. Anyway, I do wish they were marveled by some of my other abilities, but that's the subject for a different book — back to the story.

At the end of each school year, there are several dances held on campus, one of which is the "Senior Ring Dance." It is also about this time that selections are made for the outfit positions for the next year. In other words, the seniors of each outfit select which junior in the outfit is deserving to be the outfit commander for the next year. Likewise, the selection of the next year's outfit first sergeant is also determined from among the sophomores.

It is usually highly competitive, and two or three are always "in the running"; this was true in Squadron 2, for sure. To protect the identity of the two sophomores who were strongly vying to become first sergeant of Squadron 2, I will refer to them as Mr. "A" and Mr. "B." It should further be pointed out that these two "wet-heads" would not win any popularity contest if the voting were left to the fish of Gator 2. Problem was, fish never got to vote. It's just another one of those privileges that you have to earn at A&M — nothing is automatically given to you at A&M. That's another reason we're so different from a student at t.u.

For a fish to get back at a "wet-head" is an achievement that only Aggies can understand to the fullest. Suffice it to say, there is great rejoicing among all Aggie fish when a prank is pulled on one of those hard-nosed, mean, sorry, crybaby sophomores. I mean *GREAT* REJOICING!!!

Story:

I lived on the second floor two doors down from my commanding officer, Mr. Thompson, and directly across from Mr. Walton, a senior from Beaumont. My roommate was fish Music from Galveston. Mr. "A" lived on the first floor, and Mr. "B" lived down the hall on the second floor. It was supposed to be study time, and fish could not close the doors to their rooms during this period. Well, about 7:30 p.m. the night before Senior Ring Dance, Mr. Thompson brought his senior boots to my room for me to shine prior to the dance. As he was leaving the room, I asked fish Music, "Wouldn't it be good bull if I could get a sophomore to shine Mr. Thompson's boots?" Fish Music thought that would be MARVELOUS.

Mr. Thompson heard what I said and told me, "OK, fish Cox, but if you get caught, don't expect any help from me."

"Yes, sir," I replied. Since I knew (we all knew) that Mr. "A" and Mr. "B" were both badly wanting to be first sergeant, I decided to pull it on one of them. Mr. "A" became my choice — because he was the meanest "wet-head" of all time.

I took the boots down the stairs to Mr. "A's" room and knocked on the door — although the knocking of my knees might have sufficed. He opened the door and the following routine occurred:

Fish Cox: "Howdy Mr. "A," sir."

Mr. "A": "What do you want, fish Cox?"

Fish Cox: "Sir, not being informed to the . . . ."

Mr. "A": "No, really fish Cox, what are you doing with those boots?"

Fish Cox: "Mr. Thompson gave them to me to give to give to you to shine before the Senior Ring Dance, Mr. "A," sir."

Mr. "A": "Oh, he did, did he?"

Fish Cox: "Yes, sir, Mr. "A," sir!"

Mr. "A": "How come?"

Fish Cox: "Sir, not being informed . . . ."

Mr. "A": "No, really, fish Cox, why?"

Fish Cox: "Well, sir, I cogitate that Mr. Thompson is trying to decide who to pick for first sergeant, and it's between you and Mr. "B." He's having a hard time deciding, and I cogitate he wants to see if you'll do a good job on shining his boots. If you do a good job on such a small project, he

figures that you'd really do a good job on an important task,
and that would prove that you deserve to be first sergeant,
Mr. "A," sir!" (Note: I was sweating and shaking profusely
at this time.)

Mr. "A":   "Really, fish Cox, really?" (He was getting very
excited now and lost all form of cogitative reasoning.)

Fish Cox: "Yes, Sir, I cogitate so, sir!"

Mr. "A": "When did he want them back?"

Fish Cox: "Sir, not being . . ."

Mr. "A": "No, really, when?"

Fish Cox: "I cogitate by 5:00 p.m. tomorrow, Mr. "A," sir!" (I
wanted to give him plenty of time to allow me to get them
from him. I didn't want him to take them back to Mr.
Thompson because I figured he'd ask him about it.)

Mr. "A": "Thanks, fish Cox. You may leave now." (This was
the first time I ever heard him say, "Thanks," the whole
year.)

Fish Cox: "Yes sir, Mr. "A," sir."

With that, I went back to my room. The word spread
quickly among my fish buddies. We were all rejoicing over the
conquest.

In the meantime, Mr. Thompson had shared the prank with
Mr. Walton, his senior buddy. Mr. Walton thought we were
"cool." In fact, he then brought his boots to me and said, "Why
don't you try mine on someone else?"

I was feeling so good and brave by this time that I eagerly
jumped at the opportunity. This time I would take the boots to
Mr. "B." Well, I did, and the conversation was almost identical
to the conversation I had with Mr. "A." The main exception
being when Mr. "B" asked "Why?", I responded by saying
"Well, sir, Mr. Thompson gave his boots to Mr. "A," and now

Mr. Walton is giving his boots to you. I cogitate they're trying to see which of you will do the best job on this menial task, and that way they'll know who to select for first sergeant." Boy, was he ever excited. Mission accomplished. Salvo; rejoicing beyond measure.

We fish walked by Mr. "A's" and Mr. "B's" rooms several times over the next two hours. Each time, both were feverishly working on shining the boots. We loved it.

About 10:00 p.m. the same night, I was in the hall when I saw Mr. "A" strolling down the corridor with "sparkling boots" in hand and heading for Mr. Thompson's room. I tried my best to stop him by telling him Mr. Thompson didn't want to be disturbed. He did not listen, even after several repeated efforts. He continued on. I hid.

Well, I didn't know it at the time but learned later that Mr. Thompson heard my efforts to stop Mr. "A" from coming to his room. So, he was at his desk dying laughing when Mr. "A" knocked on his door. He told Mr. "A" to come in. Mr. "A" asked no questions of Mr. Thompson and left the boots and the room. Of course, this was of great comfort to me. I was able to relax for awhile. With the door open, I was sitting at my desk when I looked up and saw Mr. "B" at Mr. Walton's door with his boots glistening.

Mr. "B" said, "Here are your boots, Nick." (Nick was Mr. Walton's first name.)

Mr. Walton said, "OK, but what are you doing with them?" (My stomach sank as did the remainder of my body in my chair.)

Mr. "B" said, "Well, fish Cox gave them to me and told me that you gave them to him to give to me to shine."

Mr. Walton said, "Why, I gave those to fish Cox to shine!" Needless to say, ol' fish Cox was in trouble — BIG TIME. The next thing I knew, I had 17 pair of sophomore combat boots to shine before first call. Thanks to my fish buddies (who didn't think I was so great now), all 17 pair were ready to go by morning. The boots shined a lot more than we fish did for several days. Ah, but it was worth it all.

Yell Leaders Are Not Cheerleaders

Background:

Besides knowing all of the members in one's outfit, fish are also supposed to know all of the Aggie athletes, coaches, and Yell Leaders. The five men who wear white at football and basketball games are called Yell Leaders. For one to refer to a Yell Leader as a "cheerleader" would be a critical mistake. Normally, such a mistake is made only once.

Story:

During our senior year, Terry Bradburn and I were walking across campus the day after "All College Night." A fish (fish Jones, we'll call him) came up beside us to "whip out." He met Bradburn first. After going through the normal routine, but before he whipped out to me, Bradburn asked, "Do you know this man next to me?"

After looking me over, fish Jones replied, "No, Sir!" Bradburn then asked, "Have you ever seen him before?"

Fish Jones looked at me again and said, "No, Sir!"

As we continued to walk across campus, Bradburn asked, "Where were you last night, fish Jones?"

Jones replied correctly, "At All College Night, Sir." Bradburn responded, "And you've never seen this man?"

"No, Sir!" the freshman said, confused by the upperclassman's insistence that he might know me.

Bradburn then asked, "Don't you remember a man telling you about what it means to be an Aggie and leading us in the

The one on the left is a cheerleader
The one on the right is a yell leader
(I told you there is a difference.)

Spirit of Aggieland and explaining some of the traditions of A&M?"

A big smile came over fish Jones' face as he was finally able to respond, "Yes, Sir!"

"Now, do you know who this man is, fish Jones?," asked Bradburn.

"Yes, Sir!" he replied, looking as if he thought he would receive an award for finally knowing something.

"Well, who is he, fish Jones?" Bradburn inquired.

"He's the head cheerleader, Sir," replied fish Jones with a smile — the smile was short-lived I might add. Bradburn and I stopped in our tracks, as did fish Jones. I walked in front of fish Jones who was now standing at attention with an ever-fading smile on his face.

Standing a couple of inches from his nose with my index finger in his chest and a stern look in my eyes, I asked, "fish Jones, are you in the pep-squad?"

"No, Sir!" he answered.

I said, "I'm not a cheerleader either and don't you ever forget it! Do you understand, fish Jones?"

"Yes, Sir!" was his reply. As usual, there are some lessons we learn the "hard way." I am sure "fish Jones" never made the mistake of calling a Yell Leader a cheerleader again.

The Shot Heard 'Round The World
Background:

Randy Matson '67, as you must know, was the first human to throw the shot-put over 70 feet; he accomplished this feat at Kyle Field in the Spring of 1965. (I was there! I saw it! I'll never forget it!) He was also the 1968 Olympic Gold Medal winner.

As you can well imagine, Randy was the talk of the country and brought heaps of praise on himself and Texas A&M — not

Randy Matson sets world shot put record

only for "the shot," but also for his outstanding attitude and character. Randy is now the Executive Director of the Association of Former Students.

Story:

Johnnie Bickham, who was a fellow classmate and member of Squadron 2, went home with me the weekend after Randy threw the shot 70 feet. Johnnie was six inches shorter and 100 pounds lighter than Randy. Johnnie was also a character.

At church on Sunday morning, Johnnie introduced himself to all the kids (before the service started) as Randy Matson. He thought he was the "stuff." Yet, when it came time to fill out the visitor's card, he put down his real name. What he didn't know was that at the end of the service it was our pastor's custom to introduce the visitors and have them stand up. We were on the front row directly in front of the visiting evangelist. When they got to Bickham's name, he sat there a while realizing the truth was about to be revealed to all of those autograph-seeking youngsters. Finally, he stood up, but not nearly as tall, straight, and proud as before. As if that weren't embarrassing enough, the next event finished him off. The visiting evangelist smiled at Johnnie, who was still standing in front of the entire congregation, pointed at him, and said, "I like your tie."

Johnnie, still in a daze, thought he said, "Zip your fly." He immediately looked down at his zipper while the rest of us were rolling in the pews. Needless to say, I never took Johnnie to church with me again.

The "Culturizing" Of Aggies

Background:

Each year, several Aggie students are selected to participate in a cultural trip to broaden their educational experiences. The trips usually include visits to the opera, a play, a symphony, the zoo, and several other interesting and fascinating places in Houston and other Texas cities. The event, "MSC Spring Leadership," was, and is, the result of the efforts of John H. Lindsey `44 and his wife Sarah.

Story:

During our senior year, David Fox and I had the privilege of being selected for this experience. (I'm sure they selected us because they figured that anyone from Mart and New Boston could use some culture. Boy, were they ever right!) I had the privilege of staying in the home of the founder of "Spring Leadership," John Lindsey. Mr. and Mrs. Lindsey were perfect hosts and took us in as their own. Anyway, Fox and I sat on the front row during the symphony, which was directed by the famous Andre Previn. To say the least, Mr. Previn was very active and engrossed in his performance and work. We were so close, we could see the sweat dripping from the end of his nose. A great and rewarding time was had by all.

Being proper Ags, we wanted to share our newly found culture with our friends in the dorm back at the A&M campus. So, Fox and I decided to give a short exhibition of the symphony and opera each night in our room. However, we were able to give only one performance. The critical reviews were swift and decisive. We were "babbo-bombed" the first night. Unfortunately, there are still a few Aggies who don't appreciate real culture.

A Man's Best Friend

Background:

In ye ol' days, there were few Aggies who had a car, much less Porsches, Corvettes, etc., like the ones I see in the parking lots and garages today. In fact, most Ags used their Aggie thumbs to get them from one place to another.

Story:

One of my best Aggie buddies, John Stephens '64, did have a vehicle. I guess it was a car; it had 4 wheels anyway. He was living in Walton Hall during his second senior year. Problem was ol' John was (and is) a dog lover. In fact, he had a Blue Tick Hound that lived with him in Walton — that is, until the Housing Authority found out, and he was told that the dog had to go.

John said, "If the dog goes, I go." They called his hand and, sure enough, they both went. John found a little rent house out past the vet school which was conducive to creating a dog pound, and he soon had several dogs — male and female and, subsequently, he soon had several puppies.

Once on a trip home for the holidays, he had to take the black and brown mama hound and her nine puppies with him on his 260 mile journey home. Like I said earlier, his vehicle could hardly be called a vehicle. In fact, it probably wasn't called a vehicle when it conked out on John with about 200 miles still to traverse. Anxious to get home, and with no means of repairing his car, John stuck out the ol' thumb and prayed for a traveler to be sympathetic to his needs.

Finally, a couple stopped to give him a lift. Of course, they didn't realize when they stopped that John had 10 other passengers in the back seat of his broken down car. Reluctantly,

John told the couple of his plight. Fortunately, the man was an Aggie and his wife was a godly saint; they took the whole crew in, and John and family arrived safely home.

The Nervous Senior

Background:

Seniors (Leather Legs) are the King Pins of A&M. They have paid the price and have earned their privileges after three years of harassment and training. Seniors can do just about anything and get by with it, and they have, at times, been known to "stretch" the rules a little. Such was the case in our outfit when I was a fish.

"Beatings" and some other types of physical activities were supposed to be outlawed in the Corps. It was against "the rules," but beatings (not as bad as it sounds) did occur. Most fish even expected it and would probably have been disappointed if they were not the recipients of a few such poundings. You'd have to be an Aggie to understand. The seniors considered it training; we fish considered it torture. After all, they were preparing us for the worst of all eventualities of war — such as, becoming a prisoner of war. Anyway, most of the punishment was appropriate and carried out with the best of intentions.

Story:

Mr. Walton, a senior in Squadron 2, felt it was his personal responsibility to prepare us fish to be able to survive the roughest of all possible prisoner of war camps. He was good at his job. I had related some of the "torture" stories to my parents on occasion — especially when I needed some sympathy. Before the "Turkey Day Game" of our freshman year, we (the Corps) were preparing for the march-in in front of our dorm. My parents, along with others, were visiting and watching the outfits form-up. It was the first time we had a chance to introduce our parents to the upperclassmen.

By this time, my parents were already wondering why they were having to pay so much money for my education when it seemed as if all I were doing involved push-ups, marching bull-ring, or shining boots. Anyway, I introduced my dad to Mr. Walton. My dad then poked his finger in Mr. Walton's chest and asked, "Are you the one who's been whipping my boy?"

Mr Walton very nervously blurted out, "I guess so, sir."

My dad then said, "I want to tell you one thing, and I don't want you to forget it!" (Mr. Walton was looking more nervous by the moment.) "You aren't beating him enough!"

Mr. Walton gave a sigh of relief and, sure enough, he didn't forget to obey my dad's instructions. I knew right then that my letters requesting sympathy were falling on deaf ears with my dad. I never complained to them again.

Mascot Marauders

Background:

As you know, the t.u. mascot, Bevo, got it's name when we branded the score of our victory (13-0) on his flank. The 'sips converted the score to B-E-V-O. On several occasions, the Ags have confiscated the mascots of other SWC schools; as far as I know, we have never harmed them. In fact, our vet school has on several occasions nursed them back to health.

Story:

In the 1963-64 school year, Aggies obtained five different mascots from other schools. One of them was Bevo. We hid him out for several days until the 'sips called in the Texas Rangers and charged us with cattle rustling. We arranged for them to pick up Bevo at the vet school. When the 'sips (including their cheerleaders) arrived to haul him back, we had some fish walk a Bevo look-alike that had been de-horned around the corner of a building — you should have seen their faces! They cried and cried until we finally brought the real Bevo to them. I couldn't understand what all the fuss was about. Why, we've been sawing varsity's horns off for years.

Dad, Why Didn't You Hit Him?
Background:

Aggies aren't fond of teasips. Aggies yell for their team while the 'sips yell against their opponents. What's worse is that some teasips have a propensity for throwing ice and/or cups at Aggie players, yell leaders, the band, or anyone wearing maroon. (Evidently, most 'sips do their graduate work at LSU, where they hone these skills to perfection.)

Story:

Date: Turkey Day 1963
Place: Kyle Field
Game: Aggies (2-6-1) vs t-sips (9-0)
Situation: The 'sips, with their many liberal t.u. journalism graduates on the voting board (much like the t.u. graduates on the NCAA rules infractions committee), came into the game ranked #1 in the nation. The Ags had won only two games and were at least 30-point underdogs (something you new Ags have thankfully never experienced).

The out-manned Ags had fought their hearts out the entire game and led 13-9 with less than two minutes to go. The 'sips, who in those days had blue-chippers three deep who never

From the 1964 Aggieland

See, I told you it was an interception!

played, were driving against the Ags. With time running out, the 'sip quarterback lofted a pass into the end zone, only to have it intercepted by Aggie safety, Jim Willenborg. Willenborg caught the ball a full three feet inside the back end zone stripe. He fell to his knees (still inside the stripe) and slid out of the end zone. In what our coach called the most unjust call he had ever seen, the referee ruled the pass incomplete.

All replays, all still photos, all first-hand witnesses (including yours truly, who was stationed on the track on the end zone line) clearly reveal that the ball was legally intercepted. But, no, the ball was given back to the 'sips, who wound up scoring with a few seconds remaining. After the game, standing at attention, we (Yell Leaders) led the Twelfth Man in the singing of "The Twelfth Man." As tears were streaming down my face, a 'sip and his girlfriend walked between us and the stands. He stuck his "hook-um horns" sign in my face and laughed his sissy laugh. Oh, how I wanted to break rank, break tradition, and break his nose. The only way I can answer my son's question of "Why didn't you hit him, Dad?" is to say that our personal desires must take second place to the honored position of A&M's reputation.

The next morning's headlines, "Ags-13, Sips-9, Refs-6," did little to soothe the pain, but it did much to permanently ingrain in my mind and heart how truly different the Aggies are in comparison to the 'sips.

A final note: my son, John, did gain some measure of revenge for me some 26 years later when he was a junior in high school. It was at the 1989 A&M-t.u. game at Kyle Field. You remember — the one when the 'sip football team started a fight with our team at mid-field before the game while we were singing *The Spirit of Aggieland*. John was on the track standing on a folding chair. A Longhorn student was next to him. The 'sip started mouthing about the Ags and gave John a shove.

John, who was outweighed by about 40 pounds, came back and shoved the 'sip over two rows of chairs. Several Aggie seniors came up to John, congratulating him and patting him on the back. He was so fired up that I thought he was going to forget about finishing high school and just stay at Aggieland and major in "Whipping the 'Sips."

The Aggie Gladiators

Background:

See: "Dad, why didn't you hit him?"

Story:

Date: January 13, 1964

Place: Gregory Gym (t.u. campus)

Situation: Three hundred of us Ags traveled to Austin to watch (with 7,700 'sips) the Aggie basketball team whip the Longhorns. We had led the entire game. With about four minutes to go, Shelby Metcalf, famed Aggie basketball coach, pulled star senior and All-American Bennie Lenox to give him a rest. Our comfortable lead dwindled, and the 'sips tied us with two minutes to play.

The ice throwing started from the 'sips as they began to chant, "poor Aggies" and "choke, choke, choke." (Typical 'sip reaction.) Metcalf put Lenox back in as we 300 Aggies yelled our approval. On three straight Aggie possessions, Lenox dribbled the length of the floor, pulled up at the top of the key, and swished the net, all to the delight of us Ags. After the game, a fight ensued — much like that at the Alamo. Needless to say, we won the game, the SWC championship, and the fight all at the same time. What a day.

The headlines in the Austin paper the next day read,

"Gladiators Invade Gregory Gym." Of course, the fight was all our fault according to them. The odds, 7,700 to 300, were not good, but I'd take 'em any day as long as the 300 were Aggies. By the way, we also won the SWC Baseball Championship that same year by beating t.u. in the last game of the season on their own field. GIG'EM AGGIES!

The Flick

Background:

Guion Hall was a building located east of the MSC. It was designed with a theater type setting and was the place "Flicks" (movies) were shown from time to time. It was also the gathering place for all of the campus wits — and they were great in quantity and quality. There was a "comeback" for just about every line in the movie — especially the romantic lines — and often the remarks were more entertaining than the movies.

Story:

There were so many stories, I can't separate them enough in my memory to relay just one to you. I do remember that it was always a thrill to go to Guion Hall as it served as an escape valve from the pressures of school. It was one of my Dad's favorite places. He enjoyed the quips as much as anyone and would always wind up with "laughing tears" streaming down his face. I remember those tears, but I also remember the many grade points I lost there which brought other types of tears. What a place. Wish I could go there tonight. Don't you?

Phone Jock

Background:

In ol' army days (real ol' army days), instead of having a phone in each room, as many do now, there was one (that's right, only one) phone in the lounge for the entire four-story dorm. (I'm sure you ol' Ags of the 30's, 40's, and 50's are saying, "We didn't even have one phone in the entire Corps area.") Not only do they have phones in each room now, but they also have air conditioning, painted walls, and light bulbs bright enough to dispel darkness.

Anyway, back when there was just one phone per dorm, the room next to the lounge always belonged to a sophomore. The upperclassmen knew if they put a fish next to the lounge, they would ignore the ringing of the phone, since the chances were slim that it would be for them. Of course, the upperclassmen were smart enough to put fish in the room on the other side of the sophomores' room so that when the phone rang, the sophomores would beat on the wall of the fish next door. The fish would go answer the phone and then have to run to notify the called party. It seemed as though the call was almost always for someone on the fourth floor.

Story:

The "phone jocks" for Dorm 6 were fish Franklin and fish Frantz. Needless to say, they were the first fish to learn everyone's name and room in the dorm — they were also in better shape than the rest of us because of all that running up and down four flights of stairs. In addition, they received less sleep and had less respect and admiration for "Ma Bell" than those of us who lived further down the hall. Truthfully, I don't know how they passed their courses.

It was a nightmare. In fact, one night, fish Franklin was having a nightmare about the phone ringing. In the middle of a deep sleep, Franklin sat up in the middle of his bunk and screamed, "I'll get it!" He rolled out of bed, plunging to the floor, and hit his head on the concrete. What made it so bad was that Franklin slept in the top bunk. I've never known of anyone who enjoyed going to the hospital so much. Franklin said that not having to answer the phone was worth it all.

To this day, he doesn't answer the phone at home, and he thinks that anyone who has a car phone is a little wacky. Franklin has three sons and a wonderful wife who serve as 'phone jocks' now. Don't feel too sorry for them though because Franklin at least lets *them* sleep on the bottom bunk.

Summary

There are thousands of other stories — your stories. Remember? I know you do — stories about the Bull Ring, the deal fights, the drown-outs, the push-ups, the pink-stool, the broom, and Burning-off Your Handle. (For more stories, I recommend that you read *Good Bull: 30 Years of Aggie Escapades* and *Good Bull 2: More Aggie Escapades* by John R. Hoyle '57. Insite Press.)

Chapter 9

Aggies are Leaders

I HAVE read in publications that A&M is "striving to become" a world class institution. Texas A&M is *already* a world class university. That's not to say that those scholars of the northeastern liberal institutes of socialism nor the administrators of the California schools of extremism will ever admit that fact, but so what? Who cares? Surely, those who determine the direction of A&M's future are not of the opinion that A&M needs to become another Harvard or Yale or Berkley. Surely, we understand that the United States would be better off if the schools of the Ivy League and West Coast produced more graduates who were able to function and lead in the "real world" as do those who graduate from Aggieland. Texas A&M is special. Let it always be so!

Texas A&M affords the opportunity for all students to excel in their chosen vocation in life. We as humans are complex beings. We are physical, mental, and spiritual. Our potential is great. For the most part, however, our accomplishments are few in relation to our potential. Yet, we must continue to strive to do our best in whatever area of life we choose to serve. A college education should help us to grow in each of these three areas — mental, physical, and spiritual.

Few students at A&M participate in a varsity sport. However, all can still grow physically by participating in one of the most outstanding intramural programs in America and through a personalized work-out schedule.

Students can also grow spiritually while at A&M. There are many religious activities available to all students. For those seeking the truth, there are many Christ-centered churches and organizations in the area and on campus which will welcome any student with open arms.

And mental growth is achieved through the challenging classes the students will attend and through having the opportunity to meet fellow students from different areas of the country and world who have different backgrounds, experiences, goals, and thoughts. This, perhaps, is the most important factor in helping us to reach our full potential.

The transition from high school to college involves more than just "the next step" if that college is Texas A&M. There is much more to becoming a life-long, maroon-bleeding, fightin' Texas Aggie than just attending classes. The transition experience normally provides some anxious moments for new students whether they are going to be civilians, or members of the Corps. Change is difficult, but rewarding, if that change is to Aggieland.

Texas A&M does such a super job of insuring that this transition is carried off in a manner that is positive. The fish camps, orientation sessions, and "spend the night with the Corps" programs are led by Aggie students in a most professional and caring way. These student leaders represent the true spirit of Aggieland in a manner that is remarkable and pleasing to Ags of all ages. My admiration goes out to each of you that is actively involved in the process. Thank you for carrying on with the spirit and traditions which we hold so dear. You are Aggies in every sense of the word.

So, why is an education from A&M so special and important? We know what it will do for us personally, but surely there is more to it than that. Surely, it is more than being able to "hang a sheepskin on the wall," or to be "the first in your family to receive a college degree," or to put oneself into a position to make more money. While all of these are important, there must be more to obtaining a higher education than "what's in it for me?"

First, we owe so much to so many. Our parents, and even our grandparents, have sacrificed some of their own goals and desires in order that we may have the chance to go to college. We owe them. Not that they expect anything in return, it's just that we want to show our gratitude for them and to give them our love, respect, and honor. Second, we owe our country — the men and women of our military forces who have sacrificed their all so that we, and others, can even have a college to attend. In essence, Aggies want to do our part in repaying the debt we owe.

With all the problems related to drug abuse, the poisoning of our environment, the homeless, the handicapped, etc., . . . we must all be involved in being a part of the solution rather than a part of the problem. There is much to be done. We, as Aggies, have always wanted to do our part. An education at Texas A&M will help us reach our potential and fulfill our desire to serve mankind.

As you know, true leaders are few and far between. It is one thing to be a "Boss" and quite another to be a "Leader."

Webster defines the word "lead" as "to guide someone along a way; to go in advance; to direct on a course or in a direction." The goal of A&M is to help make each student a better leader.

At A&M, there is simply no substitute for caring, empathy, honesty, patience, fairness, sharing, listening, showing recognition to fellow Aggies. By participating in the many student organizations at Texas A&M, a student learns to:

* accept responsibility,
* work as well as lead,
* volunteer for tasks,
* be loyal,
* be emotionally mature,
* be willing to share,
* look for ways to recognize others,
* show a balance of interest in work and people,
* express a vision,
* be considerate of the needs of others, and
* have a sense of humor.

These are traits graduates of Texas A&M have exhibited over and over on the battlefield, in corporate offices, and in classrooms. It's not by accident! The emphasis comes from our parents, from the faculty, the administration, and from the thousands of Aggie students and former students. Leadership engulfs Aggieland. It permeates the air. Go ahead — take a breath and see what I mean.

Although the following letter was not written to me during my days at A&M, it well could have been; the advice is still pertinent and would be applicable for any situation, any age. I could not improve on any advice given by my father. I am proud to pass on his words of wisdom to you and especially to you young Aggies.

My mother and father never sat me down and taught me

about love — they just loved. They never talked to me about sharing — they just shared. They never explained to me about equality — they just treated everyone fairly. They never said you have to do your best — they just always went the extra mile. They led by example. As an illustration of what they believed and stood for, I am including the words my father penned to me when I was a fourteen year old boy at scout camp. (Note: My dad called me Scoot, Mr. Warren was the camp director; and the card mentioned was one of those "Do Not Disturb/Maid Service" hotel cards that you put on the door knob of your hotel room. My dad had a sense of humor to go along with his common sense — all good leaders do.)

June 18, 1957

Hi Scoot—

Sure wish I was there at old Camp Pioneer with you. I have always had a lot of fun there, and I know you will enjoy it as much as I always did. I am enclosing the card for you to hang on your bed so you can sleep as long as you wish. After you get up just turn the card over to the MAID SERVICE side and Mr. Warren will see that someone will make up your bunk for you.

Have a good time and be sure and listen and learn everything you can. I can assure you that it will come in handy one of these days.

If Mr. Stilwell comes back to camp I would like for you to introduce yourself to him and tell him that you are my boy. He has been a good friend to me, and I admire him very much. Obey your leaders, learn and know all the staff as they are outstanding young boys and men and will always be an inspiration for you. Help all the younger scouts as much as you can and this will, in turn, help you to learn more.

Give my regards to Mr. Buck, Bobby, Larry, and all the
fellows.

Be a good scout, use good common sense at all times and
remember that someone is always watching and taking care
of you.

We are very proud of you and always will be.

Your dad and pal,
Bubba

Oh to be half the Dad he was. I know you know what I mean.

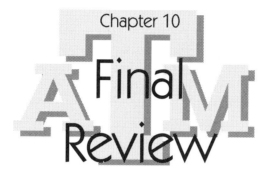

Chapter 10
Final Review

"I will be your friend forever"

FINAL REVIEW occurs in May following graduation. Two reviews are held. In the first, cadets march in the position held during the school year; then, seniors line up on the main drill field and sing "Auld Lang Syne." For the second review, cadets take the roles they will hold for the next year. Graduating seniors serve as reviewing officers for the new seniors, juniors, and sophomores as they pass in review. This is the only time that the Corps marches without a fish class.

The finality of the Review can only be understood by those who have participated in it. For the seniors to realize that Final Review is the last time they will be a part of the Corps of Cadets is a heart-wrenching experience.

Those of you who have seen the movie, "Dances With Wolves," will surely remember the final scene where Wind in His Hair holds his hand high as he watches his friend, Dances With

Wolves, ride off. Knowing of the possibility that he may never see him again, he shouts out, "Dances With Wolves, Wind In His Hair is your friend forever." Over and over he repeats it until Dances With Wolves can no longer hear him. But, oh, how it continued to ring clear in his heart, his mind, and his soul.

As I sat there, I could not help but hear the echo of similar words spoken some 25 years before at my Final Review in May of 1965. "I will be your friend forever." Only once since has a parting been so sad, so final. That was when my dad died in 1984. Gone was the best father a son could have. Yet, I still hear his words of wisdom and feel his love in my heart.

I know you have had similar experiences with your friends and family. Only Ags can know the true meaning and feeling of Final Review; the numbness, the tears, the lump in the throat, the inability to say all you desire to say — all of these feelings and more.

In 1965, many of us were going directly into the military. The Vietnam War was expanding each day. We knew there was a possibility that we would never see some of our classmates again, and the reality of the situation finally hit home for many of us. Aggies go through so much together — fish year, hazing, Bull-Ring, March-ins, Corps trips, Midnight Yell, Bonfire, Elephant Walk and, yes, Silver Taps and Muster. We had laughed and cried together. In just four short years we had become as one — closer than brothers, true friends, and comrades. We would have done anything for each other. But at Final Review we had to part — some to war, some to give the supreme sacrifice. It was the saddest day of my life. It was my *final* Final Review. There is not much more I can say about it except — Johnnie, David, Herb, Ted, Joe, Steve, Ron, Roy, George, Larry, Darryl, Chris, Gary, Bill, Rob, Rod, Maury, Cliff, Hunter, Scot, Kevin, Dan, Mark, Brian, John, Cristy ... (put your name in there)... I WILL BE YOUR FRIEND FOREVER.

I'll be your friend forever.

Chapter 11

The Journey Goes On

"...and upward"

THE BERLIN Wall has fallen; Nolan Ryan is still "throwing heat," but now it's for the Texas Rangers to the tune of more than 300 victories, more than 5,500 strike outs, and the 'magnificent seven' no-hitters; Ted Williams is still the last ball player to hit over 400; Rickey Nelson and Elvis are dead; the Corps of Cadets is optional; the late Roy Orbison still has a hit in "Pretty Woman," and Texas A&M now has not only pretty, but also intelligent and dedicated, women to go along with the men. George Bush is now working in the White House instead of the oil fields of West Texas and has a street named in his honor on the south side of campus. And, although she is now deceased, I still love Natalie Wood. Ted is now a General in the Marine Corps; David (from Houston) is an outstanding Christian witness in Kansas; David (from Mart) is a leading researcher in the agricultural field and is highly instrumental in helping feed the world; Johnnie (yes, he did graduate) is a leader in his community and the father of Brigette '92; Herb is one of those good lawyers and has lifetime tickets on the fifty yard line at Kyle Field (save me a seat); Ron is an entrepreneur in Austin (hey, they need some smart Ags in Austin); Steve influences youngsters throughout the state as a Christian disc-jockey; Larry is a fighter pilot with the Marines; Roy is an active member of his church and was selected to the Houston Bowler's Hall of Fame (now his parents know where he lost all those grade-points while at A&M); Buddy is a "Top Gun" with Mobil Oil; Malon is the fortunate one who stayed at A&M and became an Assistant to the Vice-President (he is also a tremendous help to those of us who have children who score less than 500 on the SAT — just kidding); George oversees Disney World (at least he can see it from his front porch) and, ...

The civilian student population at A&M is around 39,000, including more that 15,000 females, and the Corps, which is no longer compulsory, has around 2,000 members. There are approximately 2,500 foreign students representing more than 100 different countries on the A&M campus. And, in keeping with our mission of becoming a world-class institution, A&M now has two campuses on foreign soil; Koriyama, Japan and Castiglion Fiorentino, Italy. Guion Hall and other buildings of old have been replaced by countless new structures, including a new baseball field, track, and research park. Gas in Bryan/College Station hovers around $1.24 a gallon.

The ten colleges of A&M offer around 100 bachelor's degrees, more than 110 master's degrees, and close to 90 doctoral disciplines. A&M offers a doctor of medicine and veterinary medicine. Texas A&M University ranks among the nation's leaders in business, agriculture, engineering, architecture, and veterinary medicine schools. A&M also owns more nuclear equipment than any other school in the United States.

Texas A&M of the 90's is a far cry from the A&M of the 60's, but only in some ways. The "guts" of A&M remain the same. "All for one, one for all" is still the battle cry of Aggies. The student life is full of activities, clubs, events, and services to the university and community. Aggies are involved. We are still "doers," not just listeners. Yes, A&M is truly a world class institution. We set the standard. We always have; it's just that, now, others outside of Aggieland recognize it, too.

It's been 30 years since I first set foot on the A&M campus. It's been 60 years for some of you. Where has the time gone?

For you new Ags, I encourage you to just take advantage of it all. There is so much to do and so many good friends to make. Be more than a student. Be an Aggie. Stand tall. Be humble but strong. You are part of a special breed. Uphold the name and the spirit of Texas A&M. You are heirs of a rich history. It is your responsibility to insure that it continues. I know you will for the

Texas A&M Campus Today

cost of failing would be too great. So, take the challenge, pick up the torch, carry the spirit for the Ags of the past, for yourself, and for Ags of the future. It's up to you to do it.

One of the exceptional benefits of being an Aggie is that even after an Aggie leaves Aggieland, Aggieland never leaves the Aggie. Former students are able to continue to be a part of our great institution through participation in the Association of Former Students and the Twelfth Man Foundation. We, also, are able to contribute to the education of future Ags by funding Sul Ross Scholarships or other similar scholarships.

Aggies return to A&M not only for class reunions and ball games, but for Final Review, Parents' Weekend, Bonfire, Muster, Aggie Hostel, and just to walk around. Why, even the President of the United States of America, George Bush, has chosen Texas A&M as the home of his Presidential Library. And it is always comforting and encouraging to us Former Students to meet the new Ags. Each time my family returns to Aggieland, whether in the 70's, 80's, or 90's, we always sense and feel the Aggie Spirit. There seems always to be a steady stream of new leaders — a Wortham, a Hopgood, a Fisher, a Cleavenger, a Tisch, a Southerland, a Taylor, a Dugosh, a Moser, a Rowe, a Grimes, a Klein, a Dean, a Potter, a McGill, a Fitzgerald, a Matson, a Rudder, a Stallings, a Welch, a Garcia, a Brunner, a Sullivan, a Canter, a Bishop, a Debenport, a Morgan, a McClure, a Buckman, a Brothers, a Dutton, a Rizzo, a Youngkin, an Ince, a Reams, a Remke, a Martinez — all Aggies through and through. May it always be so. It must always be so — for my son, John, and my daughter, Cristy, for your children and our grandchildren, for Texas, for the nation, for the world.

Well, it has been great. Aren't you glad to have been a part of Aggiedom? Isn't it good to know that we'll continue to be a part of the future of Aggieland through our involvement as

Former Students. It is really kind of sad that most graduates of other schools live and die according to the accomplishments of their athletic teams. When they lose, their t-shirts, caps and stickers go in the closet. Not us! Not Aggies! While we stand with any on the athletic field, we stand above all in school pride, spirit, dedication, loyalty, and devotion. Just review the traditions, just listen to a group of Ags as they share in fellowship, just look at the gleam, and possibly a tear, in the eye of an old Ag as he sings the "Spirit," watches Final Review, or speaks of his Aggie buddies and days gone by. Then, you will understand why Aggies stick by each other. You will know why Aggies "stand united . . . ."

When the time comes to cross over to the golden shore, my last thoughts will be of Jesus and my family. But they will also be of the Corps, the Twelfth Man, marching to chow, the Quad, Yell Practice, Elephant Walk, Bonfire, ball games, sabres, senior boots, the Spirit of Aggieland. I will think of my Squadron 2 fish buddies, my many friends of Aggieland, the "War Hymn," the Bull-Ring, push-ups, cush questions, the R.V.'s, and the great traditions of A&M. Flashing through my heart and mind will be a picture of the countless Aggies who have given their all on the beaches of Normandy, the sands of Iwo Jima, the hillsides of Korea, the islands of the Pacific, the jungles of Vietnam, and the deserts of the Middle East, of the many Aggies who have received the Congressional Medal of Honor, the Purple Heart, and other campaign ribbons and badges of courage. All brave, all courageous, all servants of freedom. I will think of Silver Taps and Muster. I will think of you.

While a friend will answer "Here" when the roll is called for us at Aggie Muster, my earnest prayer is that when "the Roll is called up Yonder," you will be there to answer for yourself, because heaven would not be all that God intended it to be if you were not there.

If it weren't for heaven, Aggieland would be the place to spend eternity. If it weren't for the Holy Spirit, Aggie Spirit would be "The Spirit." And if it weren't for Jesus, you, my Aggie brothers and sisters, would be the best friends a man could have.

Now, hopefully, you understand why "I Bleed Maroon."

Muster - now

GIG 'EM! FIFTEEN FOR TEAM, FARMERS FIGHT, AND CALL IT A NIGHT!